Mel Bay Presents

A CONCISE HISTORY of JAZZ

by John Robert Brown

1 2 3 4 5 6 7 8 9 0

Visit us on the Web at www.melbay.com — E-mail us at email@melbay.com

John Robert Brown, author of *A Concise History of Jazz*, plays the saxophone and clarinet, and contributes to several music publications, including *Jazz Review*, *Classical Music* and *Libretto*. A former editor of *CASS Magazine*, the journal of the Clarinet and Saxophone Society of Great Britain, John contributed a chapter on 'The Clarinet in Jazz' to *The Cambridge Companion to the Clarinet*. He is the author of *A Concise Guide to Musical Terms*, published by Mel Bay, and *How to Play Saxophone*, published by St Martin's Press. John is a Trustee of the Jazz Development Trust, an independent body founded by John Dankworth CBE in 1997 with the sole purpose of improving the position of jazz in Britain.

After twenty-two years as a senior member of the teaching staff of Leeds College of Music, Britain's largest music conservatory, where he specialized in ensembles, harmony and jazz history, John Robert Brown is now the External Relations Consultant for the college. In this capacity he travels worldwide.

Acknowledgments

I would like to thank Dan Morgenstern, Director of the Institute of Jazz Studies, Rutgers University, Newark, New Jersey, for his friendship, for his numerous insights into historical matters, and for making many impressive photographs available. Author Will Friedwald summed up how I feel when, speaking of Dan, he observed, "He's a jazz saint." I wish I'd said that; I certainly agree.

Saxophonist Loren Schoenberg has an enthusiasm for, and knowledge of, jazz history which makes me glad that he has been appointed Executive Director of The Jazz Museum in Harlem. Loren inspired me by his many kindnesses and his practical help during the writing of this Concise History. Manfred Eicher, Founder and President of ECM Records in Munich, kindly provided a selection of photographs of ECM musicians. *Vielen Dank!*

Several other musicians have stimulated me by their knowledge, enthusiasm and friendly support. Alphabetically, they include Randy Brecker, Richard Cook, Lawrence Gushee, Dick Hawdon, Michele Law, Bryan Layton, Bruce Boyd Raeburn, Scott Robinson, Daryl Sherman, and Richard Sudhalter.

In the matter of detailed practical help, to this list should be added the library staff at Leeds College of Music, particularly David Thompson and Jay Glasby. Most of all I am indebted for the expertise of Graham and Elizabeth Wade, whose indefatigable, scrupulous and kindly efforts supported me tirelessly through the long process of editing and proofreading.

John Robert Brown
February 2004

Grateful acknowledgment is due to the following for the use of copyright material or for providing specific invaluable sources of information. The author apologizes for any inadvertent omissions from these acknowledgments. Any such errors will be corrected in future editions.

Corgi Books, London; Souvenir Press, London; Gary Giddins (Da Capo); Gunther Schuller; Richard Sudhalter (OUP); Simon and Schuster; Frederick J. Spencer (University of Mississippi Press); Gene Lees (Cassell); Dan Morgenstern; W. Royal Stokes (OUP); Peter Levinson (OUP); C. Easton (William Morrow); F. Zammarch , S. Mas (Parkside Publications, Seattle); Ted Gioia (University of California Press); Andy Hamilton (Jazz Review); T. Scott, Nat Hentoff, Nat Shapiro; Yale University Press; R. Domek (IAJE); M. Tucker (OUP); Simon Adams (Simon and Schuster); Adrian Ingram (Mel Bay); Barry Kernfeld (Macmillan); Random House; Mark Gridley (Prentice Hall); Quincy Troupe (Picador); Larry Fisher (Edwin Mellen Press); Mike Zwerin; Nigel Kennedy (Weidenfeld and Nicolson).

Foreword

This book, intended for the general public, music students, and enthusiasts of all ages, explores the history of jazz, its personalities and genres, from early developments to the present day.

John Robert Brown, jazz performer and jazz educator, has written an inspiring guide to a brilliantly dynamic art form which began in the USA and, within a short span of years, captivated the imagination of the entire world. John has distilled his long experience of playing and teaching jazz to interpret its complex history with clarity, enthusiasm and insight.

We would like to express our gratitude to William Bay and all his staff at Mel Bay Publications Inc., for making this book possible and to Elizabeth Wade for her invaluable editorial assistance during the preparation of this work.

Graham Wade
General Editor - ALL ABOUT MUSIC SERIES

Contents

*Pencil drawing on first page of
Lionel Hampton by
John Robert Brown.*

1. Won't You Come Along With Me?
Up the Mississippi

At dawn the river freighters glide through the lifting mist. Soon, temperatures will be high. New Orleans, boasting banana trees, palms, pink ibis and white pelicans, shares the same southerly latitude as Cairo in Egypt.

The Mississippi is gigantic; at 3,700 miles it is the fourth longest river in the world. In New Orleans, the largest raw materials port on earth, the river - 'Big Muddy' - is one third of a mile wide and two hundred feet deep. No bridge existed here until 1935. Seagoing freighters and tankers arrive from the ocean to cruise northwards through North America. Life up that lazy river had, and retains, a great commercial and social significance.

The Mississippi winds between levees, the raised banks which protect the rich farm land from flooding. Baton Rouge, Vicksburg, Memphis, St. Louis, Davenport, St. Paul and Minneapolis are all on the river. Paddle steamers which plied between these cities once employed famous New Orleans jazz musicians to entertain passengers. Even the great Louis Armstrong worked on a riverboat early in his career.

The plantations, enormous farming estates, begin only a short distance upriver. They hold the secrets to understanding the South and the Crescent City. Originally, indigo dye was harvested from cotton. Later, sugar, cotton and maize were produced.

Presiding over one of the largest plantations, Houmas House, sixty miles from New Orleans, is typical. A beautiful antebellum mansion in Greek revival style, at its zenith the estate of this grand dame of the great river road had 30,000 acres of land, originally purchased at four cents an acre. Houmas plantation, the prime sugar producer in America, required a vast work force. One thousand slaves worked here.

It is difficult to imagine what daily life was like for the slaves. At Houmas House, with its gorgeous gardens and gazebos, you will see nothing of the slaves' accommodation. However, the intriguing *garçonnières* still stand nearby. The name derives from *garçon*, which is French for boy. Garçonnières are small houses built onto the side of the mansion. They were provided as bachelor housing for the planter's son, who had come of age but was yet to marry.

Down the grass bank of the levee outside the gates to Houmas House, Old Man River still rolls along, bringing cargo ships and tankers to ten states. Above, away from the river, is the Houmas mansion. Surrounded by lawns, today the house is beautifully maintained, her cream walls and elegant columns visible behind the ancient trees.

The South before 1917 - The People and the Place

The South consisted of the states of Alabama, Arkansas, Florida, Georgia, Louisiana, Mississippi, North Carolina, South Carolina, Tennessee, Texas and Virginia. The Southern economy was based on slave labor. During the 1840s and 1850s these states wanted to extend slavery westwards. The North, which had a growing economy based on manufacturing and small farms, called for abolition. The Civil War (1861-1865) between the Unionist Northern States and the Confederate Southern States was fought over the issue of slavery and the related matters of trade and tariffs. With the Unionist victory in

1865, complete liberation from slavery (manumission) was achieved. The abolition of slavery made jazz possible.

Black slaves were first brought to New Orleans by the French in 1719. Not all blacks were slaves. There were free blacks in the south as early as 1722. Altogether nearly half a million slaves were imported into North America, mostly from the West Indies but also from Africa. Some were from the interior of the American South. The island of Cuba lies only ninety miles from the coast of Florida. Here the sugar industry boomed. Six hundred thousand slaves were said to have been brought to Cuba from the Old World, between 1800 and 1865. Their descendants still work in the Cuban cane fields today.

By 1808 the importation of slaves was made illegal in the United States. Those already there remained as slaves.

Early jazz musicians, such as Sidney Bechet, Johnny Dodds, Alphonse Picou, Jelly Roll Morton and Kid Ory, were Creoles. 'Creole' is a confusing and imprecise word. Many types of Creoles have existed, black and white, rural and urban. The word originally came from Spanish or Portuguese, meaning 'Native to the New World'. By the time of the Civil War it had come to mean 'Native to Louisiana', describing any native, regardless of color. The first whites born in New Orleans, mostly of French descent, were the first folk to be known as Creoles.

At the end of the nineteenth century the Creoles were either free blacks or persons of mixed race. They spoke French or Spanish, and came originally from the West Indies. Today, black Creoles in Southwest Louisiana have monopolized the term. A modern definition of Creole would be 'a black or mixed-race person, of French heritage and usually of Catholic faith'.

A hierarchy based on skin color (pigmentocracy) existed in the South after the introduction of slavery. The nearer a slave's looks approached those of a European, the better the job he was given. A slave's appearance alone could secure work in the master's house, an escape from toiling in the fields.

The nineteenth century Creoles in New Orleans (free blacks or persons of mixed race) regarded themselves as superior to other racial groups. At the time of the birth of jazz they were well educated, successful, business people or craftsmen, and spoke French. Many of these Creoles owned slaves. The Creoles lived in the area known today as the French Quarter. Most Negroes lived uptown, and were employed as laborers.

Skin color is also relevant to the term Dixieland, which dates from the time of French rule during the forty years after the city was founded in 1718. Originally the word described a geographical area, not a type of music. The words *Dixie* and *Dixieland* had been used as synonyms for the South since before the Civil War. Some argue that Dixieland derives from the Louisiana ten-dollar bill, with the value printed in French, *dix*. Others claim that the term comes from the Mason-Dixon Line, drawn up by two English astronomers, Charles Mason and Jeremiah Dixon, who conducted a survey between 1763 and 1767. The line was the geographical boundary between Pennsylvania and Maryland, the border dividing the slave states from the free states. To this day, the boundary distinguishes the North from the South. Dixieland Jazz is the term used to describe vintage jazz played by the classic New Orleans front line of clarinet, trumpet and trombone.

It is important to understand that originally there was a racial implication, as the term Dixieland should only be applied to white bands from those eleven southern states that left the Union in 1861 rather than abolish slavery. Some would regard it as offensive to describe black bands from this area as 'Dixieland' bands.

For a long while, a safer title was 'traditional', or 'trad' jazz. But words continue to change meaning. From the 1980s onwards it was noticeable that young people used the term 'traditional jazz' to refer to any jazz that did not have even eight-in-a-bar rock rhythms. To an older person it sounded bizarre to hear anything that swung - a big band, or an Art Blakey - style hard bop combo - described as traditional jazz!

Music entered the daily toil of gangs of laborers as work songs. Before the introduction of machinery, heavy work was done by teams of men or by draft animals. The chanting of a work song, often in call and answer style (antiphony), was an aid to cohesion. This was the method of coordinating the drag on a rope, the thrust of a saw, or the haul on a capstan. The word 'stevedore' comes from the Spanish, *estibador*, a packer. Black stevedores in the port of New Orleans would sing rhythmically to direct the dockers. An early jazz tune, *Stevedore Stomp*, was inspired by such a work song. Another manifestation of antiphony was in the Baptist church, the call and response between preacher and congregation.

At first, slaves were not allowed instruments. Singing was the sole means of making music. The managers feared that slaves would signal rebellious messages, especially if drums were beaten. Gradually these fears waned, replaced by the belief that singing signified serenity and satisfaction. Some songs had a strong, undiluted, African origin, including those from the tradition of the griot ('gree-oh'), the tribal historian or storyteller. Recordings made by the song collector Alan Lomax (1915-2002) revealed that some songs being sung in North

American prisons in the 1960s were almost unchanged from native songs still performed in West Africa. Away from the plantations, the great instrumental styles of the time were the cakewalk, followed by ragtime, both initially played on the piano. The name 'ragtime' comes from 'ragged time.' Ragtime, which is composed piano music printed and published for the domestic market, enjoyed substantial commercial popularity - a craze - during the years between 1890 and 1918.

At that time, domestic music-making was still important. Every middle class home had a piano. Sales of sheet music were high. The *Bunny Hug, Chicago, Grizzly Bear, Foxtrot, Texas Tommy, Turkey Trot* and the *Tango* were the popular dances of the day. Some of these dances were disliked by the older generations of the white middle class. They were seen as Africanizing American culture. The tango, still danced today, was banned by Kaiser Wilhelm in Germany, and denounced by the Pope as a pagan attack on family life.

When she first saw the tango performed in Paris in 1913, Comtesse Mélanie de Pourtales asked disingenuously whether one was supposed to dance it standing up. Libidinous and dramatic when performed well, the tango evokes the old notion that dancing is the vertical expression of a horizontal desire.

Ragtime has a strong rhythmic forward motion, with simple syncopated melodies. Syncopation is an effect of rhythmic displacement by emphasizing weak beats or weaker parts of beats. The forward motion of ragtime is achieved on the piano by a left hand 'um- cha' that alternates note and chord, in a style called stride. The um-cha style is a derivation of piano left-hand techniques that had already been brilliantly conceived and refined in Europe by Frédéric Chopin (1810-1849) and Franz Liszt (1811-1886).

Important ragtime composers were Joseph F. Lamb (1887-1960) and James Scott (1885-1938), but the foremost composer of ragtime was the American Negro, Scott Joplin (1868-1917). His *Maple Leaf Rag* was published in 1899, *The Entertainer* in 1902, the latter selling more than a million copies of printed music. Joplin wrote a rag opera, *A Guest of Honor*, in 1903, and published *Treemonisha*, another opera, in 1911. *Treemonisha* had only one concert performance during Joplin's lifetime, in 1915 at the Lincoln Theater in Harlem. It was a disaster. The opera had to wait until 1972, long after Joplin's death, for its first professional performance.

The influence of ragtime and cakewalk was sensational and global. One of the earliest recordings appeared in Sweden, *Cake Walk*, by the Kronoberg Society Regimental Band conducted by Erik Högberg, in 1899.[1] Claude Debussy (1862-1918) published *Golliwogg's Cakewalk* for piano in 1908. He had heard the band of John Philip Sousa (1854-1932) perform a cakewalk at the 1900 Paris Exposition. Irving Berlin's hit song *Alexander's Ragtime Band* appeared in 1911; Igor Stravinsky published *Ragtime*, for eleven instruments, in 1918.

Early jazz performances of rags include Louis Armstrong and Earl Hines's *Weather Bird Rag*, Sidney Bechet's recording of Joplin's *Maple Leaf Rag*, Jelly Roll Morton's *Frog-I-More Rag* and Duke Ellington's first composition, *Soda Fountain Rag*. The popularity of ragtime increased interest in the piano, and created a circle of players in New Orleans.

Ragtime enjoyed a revival in 1970 when pianist Joshua Rifkin began recording immaculate and sensitive versions of many of Joplin's compositions. Subsequently, Scott Joplin's music was used on the soundtrack of the 1973 movie *The Sting*. This interest in reviving

Joplin's work occurred coincidentally with the expiry of the copyright on Joplin's performance royalties!

"New Orleans was the stomping ground for all the greatest pianists in the country," said Jelly Roll Morton. "We had Spanish, we had colored, we had white, we had Frenchmen, we had Americans, we had them from all parts of the world... The sporting houses needed professors, and we had so many different styles that whenever you came to New Orleans, it wouldn't make any difference that you just came from Paris, or any part of England, Europe, or anyplace - whatever your tunes were over there, we played them in New Orleans."[2]

The piano was not the only source of live music. In 1898 the Spanish-American War ended. The military bands were redundant, with the result that there was a plentiful supply of wind instruments available in the South - brass, woodwind and also percussion.

Therefore, it is no accident that the important front line instruments in early jazz bands are cornet, clarinet and trombone. The marching percussion instruments are also directly linked to the drum set that appeared in early jazz.

"There were always so many musicians," said Danny Barker. "Part of it was due to the fact that in New Orleans we had more access to instruments, where other parts of the South didn't. After the Spanish-American War, most of the Army bands disbanded in New Orleans, and so the pawnshops were loaded with instruments." [3]

Thus the military band had a great influence on jazz, and not only because of its instruments. Early bands played marches, such as *High Society March*, *Bourbon Street Parade* and *Under the Double Eagle*.

The form of some rags and early jazz compositions was clearly influenced by the style and structure of the march, with its trio section played in the subdominant, that is, in a key four diatonic steps above the home key.

At that time, wind bands existed to play rhythmic music for entertainment and dancing. It has been estimated that as many as sixty such bands were playing nightly for entertainment along the shores of Lake Pontchartrain in New Orleans, around 1900. [4] These were not jazz bands. Containing fifteen to twenty players, mostly wind and brass, but maybe with one or two strings and possibly a singer - together with a rudimentary rhythm section - in style they were somewhere between a military band and an early dance band. The musicians played from publishers' orchestrations, and there was little or no improvising. Such bands provided a valuable source of work for local musicians, yet their contribution is usually ignored in the story of the birth of jazz. They played the music of Sousa, orchestrations of rags and cakewalks, and they accompanied singers.

Other European music influenced jazz. Bunk Johnson (1889-1949) has spoken of the influence of the quadrille. "I was crazy to play quadrilles," he said,[5] telling how, in the 1890s, Buddy Bolden would play a quadrille that was later taken by the Original Dixieland Jazz Band (ODJB) and turned into *Tiger Rag*. Thus, the South was a musical melting pot, where European minuets, marches and opera selections existed alongside African voodoo music, and the blues. Voodoo is an Afro-Caribbean religion, a fusion of the beliefs of different racial and religious groups, its practice kept secret from the slave owners.

The blues must not be omitted from any account of how jazz began. The word is used to describe a song form, the 12 bar blues. The simplest blues uses only three chords, the primary triads. In the key of C major, these would be chords one, four and five: C, F and G7. Many blues melodies are pentatonic, that is, they use a five-note scale. 'Blues' is also a description of a mood or a feeling, though a blues may be performed quickly in a light-hearted way. The blues tells an entirely personal story; it can be about any subject. When 'blues inflections' are discussed, this refers in part to the approximately flattened third and seventh of each chord, used to darken the major tonality and add expression. Blues performances are usually improvised.

Musicologists collected no examples of the blues until the 1920s, after the ODJB had recorded *Livery Stable Blues,* a tune which has a more sophisticated chord progression, going beyond the primary triads. Later in jazz history, the blues could have any number of identities. Critic Gary Giddins was correct to observe that : "'Blues' has too many definitions." [6] Eventually, after 1940, the bebop era produced blues compositions that were rich in chromaticism. Many have two chords per bar, played in tempo and mood anything but blue.

Most remarks about the origins of the blues are speculative, though it is safe to conclude that the blues arrived in New Orleans from the Mississippi Delta sometime in the late nineteenth century. While it is reasonable to conclude that the rural blues - sung solo or with a guitar accompaniment - existed at least from the mid-nineteenth century, it is by no means certain. The commonly heard opinion that: 'First came the blues, then came jazz,' is, at best, an oversimplification. As yet, we do not know. "Blues music is a mystery to the natives," said Albert Murray. [7] Even today, when musicians assemble for a jam session, a blues still represents simple common repertoire for strangers to play together.

References

1. Nicholson, S., *Jazz Review*.
2. Shapiro, N. and Hentoff, N., *Hear Me Talkin' to Ya* (London: Souvenir Press, 1992), pp.53-54.
3. Ibid., p. 66.
4. http://www.basinstreet.com/Early-Jazz-Band.html
5. Shapiro, N. and Hentoff, N., op cit., p. 36.
6. Giddins, G., *Riding on a Blue Note* (Da Capo, 2000) p. xvi.
7. Ibid., p. xv.

2. Way Down Yonder
New Orleans before 1917

Canal Street, historically the division between the French and American parts of town, is still the boundary between uptown and downtown. During the nineteenth century, the Creoles lived in the French section. On the other side of Canal Street lay the part of town inhabited by the newly freed slaves. Storyville, the tenderloin or red light district, was positioned on the north side of Canal Street. Many of the street names are familiar to anyone with an interest in jazz. Take a closer walk, directing your feet to the sunny side, along streets that are tune titles: Perdido Street, Canal Street, South Rampart Street and Bourbon Street.

The area called the birthplace of jazz, a center of barber shops, social clubs, bakeries, pawnbrokers and saloons, where musicians met during the first years of the twentieth century, was 'back-of-town'. Here, in 1909, was founded the Zulu Social Aid and Pleasure Club. For a small subscription, members received financial help when sick, or aid when burying deceased colleagues.

Now, at the start of the twenty-first century, the area is a car park adjacent to the Holiday Inn Hotel. A realistic mural of a giant *trompe l'oeil* clarinet, fourteen stories high, is painted on the hotel, in celebration of the district's history. The Zulu organization still exists today, putting no fewer than thirty floats in the New Orleans Mardi Gras carnival each year, when it gives out more than 100,000 souvenir coconuts.

The music that was played in each community in New Orleans echoed the characteristics of the residents. Creoles were proud of their European heritage, their appreciation of waltzes, marches and opera, their thorough musical precision. By contrast, the music of the newly freed slaves on the other side of Canal Street was simpler, based on work songs or traditional melodies, performed from memory or improvised.

The important stimulus to jazz musicians leaving New Orleans, and thus spreading the music beyond the city, was the closing of the entertainment district, Storyville, in 1917. By then, people had already begun to leave the city for the north, principally Chicago. The great influx into Chicago took place between 1916 and 1919.

Unfortunately, no recordings of early jazz occurred in New Orleans. All the recordings of New Orleans jazz musicians were made in Chicago, after 1917.

Social intermingling of the races in New Orleans occurred as long ago as the beginning of the nineteenth century. Definitions of racial origins were precise. A quadroon was a person having one-quarter African blood and three-quarters Caucasian blood. An octoroon was a person one-eighth black. Quadroon balls, attended only by quadroon women and white men, were a significant part of the Carnival season for half a century. They remained largely a Creole celebration for several decades after the 1803 Louisiana Purchase, when the USA was thereby doubled in size and New Orleans became an American city.

The placage is an unconventional local tradition that has grown from quadroon balls. In a placage arrangement, a quadroon mistress would be kept by a white man, who set her up in a small dwelling, and provided for any resulting children. These children entered a privileged class of 'people of color'.

Prostitution was another notable factor in the birth of jazz. Since

1857, the city had one of the largest and most famous legalized brothel districts in America, important to the sailors in the adjacent US naval base, to other visitors, and to the economy of the city. While prostitution may have been enjoyable for the sailors, it lessened their fitness for work. Alderman Joseph Story therefore attempted to limit prostitution to one section of town. This section, 'The District', became known as Storyville.

Among the many musicians working in 'NawLeans', the one most surrounded by myth and legend is Charles 'Buddy' Bolden. Born in 1877, Bolden took up the cornet around 1894. By 1895 he was leading his own semi-professional group, and by 1901 his group had stabilized into a six-piece unit with cornet, clarinet, valve trombone, guitar, double bass, and drums - a combination of instruments that was decidedly 'modern', and would not have sounded out of place if specified for a 1950s cool jazz combo.

Bolden's rise to fame coincided with the emergence of the Storyville district, where he soon became a local celebrity. By 1905, when his fame was at its peak, Bolden's group performed regularly in the city's dance halls and parks, and undertook excursions to outlying towns. In the following year, Bolden showed clear signs of violent mental derangement. His band rapidly collapsed. In 1907, in a state of distress and alcoholism, Bolden was admitted to a mental institution in Jackson, where he remained until he died in 1931. Michael Ondaatje's novel *Coming through Slaughter* (New York, 1976) is based on Bolden's life.

In New Orleans there was a band for every occasion, be it party, parade or funeral. Guitarist Danny Barker recalled that it was common to see funerals with three or four bands in the procession. "A member probably was active in eight to twelve organizations," he said. "Masons, Odd Fellows, Tulane Club or Zulu Club, the Vidalia,

Veterans, Charity and a few more. It was more than likely his request to be buried as he lived, among a crowd and lots of music." [1]

Trumpeter Wingy Manone added: "On the way to the graveyard, they all walked slowly, following the cornet player. The cornet player was the boss. Sometimes it took them four hours to get to the cemetery. All the way they just swayed to the music and moaned." [2] On the return journey the band would swing hard, playing as hot as they knew. Recalling these scenes long afterwards for the excellent *Hear Me Talkin' to Ya*, clarinetist Edmond Hall was careful to explain that at New Orleans funerals the bands themselves never went into the cemeteries. [3]

Louis Armstrong played in Storyville as a teenager: "There was so much good music that was played in Storyville," he said. "They talked about it and its musicians until the word 'District' being used so much wouldn't sound so good. Storyville has been discussed in colleges and some of the largest universities in the world. If not all over the world. I'll bet right now most of the youngsters and hot club fans who hear the name Storyville hasn't the least idea that it consisted of some of the biggest prostitutes in the world. Standing in their doorways nightly in their fine and beautiful negligees - faintly calling to the boys as they passed their cribs. Storyville was kind of divided - I'd say - about middle ways of the City of New Orleans. Canal Street was the dividing line between the uptown and the downtown section. And right behind Canal Street was Storyville. And right off Canal Street was the famous Basin Street which was also connected with Storyville. And somewheres in or near Storyville was a famous gambling joint called Twenty-Five. That was the place where all the big-time pimps and hustlers would congregate and play 'Cotch' (that's a game they played with three cards shuffled and dealt from the bottom of the deck). And you could win or lose a whole gang of money. These pimps and hustlers, et cetera, would spend most of their time at Twenty-Five until their girls would finish turning tricks in their cribs. Then they would meet them and check up on the night's take.

"Lot of the prostitutes lived in different sections of the city and would come down to Storyville just like they had a job. There were different shifts for them. Sometimes - two prostitutes would share the rent in the same crib together. One would work in the day and the other would beat out that night shift. And business was so good in those days with the fleet of sailors and the crews from those big ships that come in from the Mississippi River from all over the world - kept them very very busy." [4]

"Keppard and others practiced at the Twenty-Five Club in New Orleans. They would all go down there after they got through with their jobs, late at night. I would play over the new pieces because I could read," said Richard M. Jones. "Then some other pianist would get up and try to play it; perhaps he could play it a little better. But they would forget it before they got through and would have to fill in with a break and other stuff. That's where the improvisation came from. They had nothing to do all day but play checkers, so they couldn't help learning their instruments. There were no schools. If they wanted to take up an instrument, they had all the time in the world to perfect their playing." [5]

In 1917, by order of the Secretary of the Navy, came the death march of the red light district; Storyville was closed. "Before they clamped down on Storyville there were an awful lot of killings going on," said Louis Armstrong. "Mysterious ones too. Several sailors were all messed up - robbed and killed. That's one of the main reasons for the closing of Storyville. Those prostitutes commenced to having their pimps hide somewheres around and either rob or bash their brains in, anything to get that money. That's when the United States Navy commenced to getting warm. That meant trouble and more trouble, not only for the vice displayers but for all the poor working people who made their living in Storyville." [6]

Although Storyville was history, prostitution still continued in New Orleans after 1917. Now it flourished all over the city. It became less overt. There was no standing in doors anymore. Prices were lower. Yet still musicians worked, in cabarets, roadhouses, vaudeville shows, circuses, on the boats at Lake Pontchartrain and in entertainment premises on the waterfront. Road bands traveled out to Mississippi, Alabama, Georgia, Florida and Louisiana.

Up the river, plantations like the one presided over by Houmas House were witness to the paddle steamers passing by. "In 1907 Fate Marable came out of Paducah, Kentucky, and started to work with me on the steamer J. S.," said Tony Catalano. "...Those boats were responsible for the start of many a famous musician as Fate, Louis Armstrong, Joe King Oliver, the Dodds Brothers and others. About 1919, Fate dropped in at a dance in New Orleans at the Cooperative Hall and heard Kid Ory's Band playing *Honky-Tonk Town* by Chris Smith. Fate asked who was playing the trumpet. It turned out to be Louis Armstrong. Bob Lyons was managing the band and playing bass. Fate went up to Lyons and asked if he could use the trumpet man... That's how Louis got his start to get out and go north, as Fate gave him steady work on the Capitol of the Streckfus Lines." [7] Thus, even before Storyville was closed, musicians were leaving New Orleans. The most popular destination for the young jazz musician was Chicago. Many New Orleans jazzmen were recorded there, later.

Recordings have been crucial in jazz history. Without recordings, the dissemination of jazz around the world could not have taken place at anything like the speed it did. Nevertheless, sound recording came slightly too late. A frustrating gap exists at the beginning of jazz history, where one can only guess at what has been missed.

Thomas Edison built the first sound-recording apparatus in 1877. By 1888 the phonograph had been developed for use as an office dictation machine. A commercial failure, early cylinder recorders were too frail for heavy use. The rough treatment received at the hands of stenographers, concerned about a threat to their profession, sabotaged the machines. The companies making them turned to other uses for their invention. Only then did the phonograph become a medium for entertainment.

Two coin-operated cylinder playback phonographs were set up in the Palais Royale Saloon in San Francisco in 1889. Such machines were at first fitted with battery driven motors, later with a spring drive. Listening was done through tubes (a distant predecessor of the earpieces on today's personal Discman or MP3 player). This enhanced the impact of the first experience of recorded sound.

The machines were small automatic phonographs that played one cylinder. Placed in amusement parks, cafés, ferryboat landings, hotels and railway stations, they were immediately successful. By 1893 they were being located together in what was known as a phonograph parlor. Later they were situated in penny vaudevilles, or penny arcades, alongside peephole machines, talk-your-weight devices, player pianos and other catchpenny contraptions.

Wind instruments recorded more effectively than strings. As a result, military-style wind ensembles and dance music dominated the record catalogs before World War I. The recordings available included vaudeville vocalists, comedians, and instrumentalists - again, usually wind players. The recording process could only cope with small ensembles, fifteen musicians or fewer, in performances shorter than three minutes. Nothing was recorded that represented the concert hall, nothing highbrow. The musical fare was that of a small town band concert.

Thus, jazz was late coming to the attention of the recording companies. For the jazz historian searching this period for clues as to how jazz came about, it is disappointing that thirty years of commercial sound recording took place before much jazz was recorded. Remember that in the early days of the phonograph a recording was an actual performance, not the step-by-step concoction that was commonplace with the arrival of magnetic tape after World War II.

Freddie Keppard and his band were the first jazz musicians to be offered the opportunity to record, by the Victor company. Several accounts exist to explain what happened. In a private email, historian Lawrence Gushee explained: "There really is no good way to choose between the various stories. One, from Bill Johnson, is that a test was made but the string bass overloaded the grooves. Baquet indicates (if you can believe Danny Barker) that the band was offended by the terms of the contract. Like virtually all such contracts, the publisher is favored. Then there's the version that Freddy wouldn't play (even for a test) without being paid."

Whichever story is correct, or whether the oft-quoted tale that Keppard was concerned about other musicians copying what he played (to the extent that he draped a handkerchief over his fingers), there was no recording for the Victor Talking Machine Company.

The first recorded jazz ensemble, therefore, was the Original

Dixieland Jazz Band (ODJB), five white musicians from New Orleans, who recorded on 26 February, 1917, shortly after their arrival in New York to undertake a residency at the 400 Room of Reisenweber's Restaurant on Columbus Circle. The ODJB's cornet player Nick LaRocca had left New Orleans for Chicago in 1916. Titles recorded in New York included their own compositions *Livery Stable Blues* and *Dixieland Jazz Band One-Step*. The recordings of the ODJB were all issued on large 12 inch discs. The ephemeral became the enduring.

The discs were surprisingly expensive. The retail price, about fifty cents, was the equivalent of one sixth of the "comfortable weekly wage for many older employees." [8]

The musicians were young. Cornetist Nick LaRocca (1889-1961) was 28, clarinetist Larry Shields 23, pianist Henry Ragas 26, trombonist Edwin 'Eddie' Edwards 26, drummer Tony Sbarbaro only 19. From the recording it is clear that, young as they were at the time, the ODJB musicians were stylistically polished, despite criticism by some commentators that the playing was crude.

Seven to ten days were spent rehearsing before the recording was made. The recorded performances contain many techniques and expressive touches that have endured in jazz, including comedy effects. Rooster cries are played on the clarinet, horse whinnies on the cornet, glissandi on the trombone and clarinet. We hear blue notes, and the twelve bar blues, colored by a progression that included cyclic harmony and a diminished chord. A kazoo was inserted in the trombone bell to make an unusual tone color on *Crazy Blues* and *Some of These Days*. Some tunes were played especially fast to fit one side of a record.

Try to hear *Livery Stable Blues* by the ODJB. The counterpoint between the three front line instruments is simply organized to avoid collisions and duplications. The considerable amount of repetition by each instrument signals that this is a well-rehearsed ensemble, even if we had not been told so by LaRocca's subsequent statements. Perfection does not happen by accident.

The influence of European marches, Sousa's American marches, and European dance music, is clear. Patterns from military drumming can be heard on the 1917 recording of *Original Dixie Jazz Band One-Step*, or the 1918 *Clarinet Marmalade* recording. Sbarbaro uses the trap set of the era, with cowbell and gong, but without a hi-hat. Nick LaRocca later told how he took, "a few bars of *The Holy City*, a few more of *La Paloma*, a snatch of the *National Emblem March* and put them together to make *Tiger Rag*." [9] LaRocca also told British writer Brian Rust that he had worked as an electrician in the Opera House on Royal Street, New Orleans. He was able to "observe closely the arias, duets and concert items being rehearsed on stage while he worked at his job". [9]

Without detracting in any way from the achievements of the five musicians of the ODJB, who have suffered more than their fair share of criticism, common sense would suggest that not all of the devices one hears on these first jazz recordings were the ODJB's original creations.

The music is a blending of many influences. The blacks had the tradition of the blues and rhythms from Africa, though several observers have remarked that, in common with much early jazz, the ODJB's music does not sound very African. The Creoles had instruments, harmony and repertoire from Europe. Nonetheless, what the preceding evolutionary stages were, and how the ODJB came to develop their sensational individual styles, is not known.

In a revelatory interview with the British journalist Max Jones, the trumpet player Wingy Manone (1900-1982) said that growing up in New Orleans he had listened to Nick LaRocca before he listened to Louis Armstrong. Asked if he heard much of LaRocca and the ODJB, he said: "Not so much. I was in short pants, you see, and had to put on long pants to get into places they played - honky tonks and whore houses in the district. They didn't make their name in New Orleans; they didn't even make it in Chicago or New York. They made their name here in London. Then they returned and went to Coney Island. I remember this: Nick had a good tone, and he knew how to swing that lead without getting lost. I got some of the records at home. I'll tell you another thing, the Dixieland Band created all those tunes themselves. You know where from? From operas. Nick took all those different strains from operas and then the band jazzed them up. They were the ones who started it all, if you want to know. Yes, started jazz. I know it, because we heard them before anyone else." [10]

On the subject of opera, it is relevant to note that when the Victor Talking Machine Company introduced the Victrola in 1901, the Italian tenor, Enrico Caruso, was a popular recording artist, alongside Sousa. In the decades before the Civil War, New Orleans had three opera companies. The influence of opera on jazz still awaits exploration.

In contrast to Wingy Manone's statement, the Creole clarinetist Paul Barnes (1901-1981), who began to listen to jazz in New Orleans just before the start of the Great War in 1914, refuted the claims that the ODJB were the originators of jazz, implying instead that they had copied others: "They weren't even playing that kind of music. That came from way back, from Buddy Bolden and Jelly Roll Morton, from King Oliver." [11] Nevertheless, Barnes granted that the ODJB was first class.

The early jazz expert Brian Rust takes the opposite view: "It has often - too often - been claimed that the Original Dixieland Jazz Band were not the originators of jazz, that there were other (mainly black) bands playing in that idiom before them. If that were so, is it not strange that these allegedly superior bands were not noticed by an alert-eared impresario and given the chance to record? That the bands existed is not in doubt; what they played was probably a form of rag-time, and if the survivors whose resurrection in the 1940s is any yard-stick, it is not surprising that they did not make some deep, indelible impression that the ODJB did. Nick LaRocca was the first to agree that jazz could develop without losing its essential basic elements. 'I think the world of Louis Armstrong and all those great men who took jazz and carried it far, but I still say we were the first'."[12]

What is beyond dispute is that the ODJB itself was immeasurably influential. The first record became an immediate hit. Even if the record did cost the equivalent of a day's pay, initially it sold 250,000 copies, more than any record before. The disc went on to sell millions. The tragic trumpeter Buddy Bolden *may* have started it all, but the ODJB recording was the first jazz that most Americans heard.

Bix Beiderbecke was so inspired by the ODJB's recordings that he bought a cornet. He taught himself to play in a style patterned on Nick LaRocca's. Other young players whose lives were changed by the band's recordings included multi-instrumentalist Brad Gowans, clar-inetist Buster Bailey, and trombonist Miff Mole. Trumpeter Phil Napoleon (1901-1990) was inspired to form an influential 'five' of his own, the Memphis Five, in 1917. The jazz craze blew quickly around the world. As early as 1921, "a New York City ordnance decreed that jazz was not to be played in nightclubs or elsewhere on Broadway after midnight, in response to vigorous protests in press and pulpit that jazz and the dancing it stimulated was 'degenerate' and 'immoral'. Victor saw to it that there were to be no more jazz records in its catalog." [13]

Unfortunately, some critics and commentators still deride or ignore the achievements of the ODJB. The band has been described as 'crude,' 'blunt,' 'second-rate' and 'watered down.' [14] This is unfair. Second rate to what? Watered down from what? Without recordings by their predecessors, we cannot say. Brian Rust made the point well: "The inescapable truth is that anything remotely recognizable as jazz that existed before the Original Dixieland Jazz Band made its debut in 1916 was never recorded under that or any other name until the ODJB made its first records on February 26, 1917." [15] Nevertheless, many historians emphasize the Afro-American origins of jazz, not accepting Rust's opinion as definitive.

After the ODJB's New York engagement and phonograph recording, the five musicians traveled to London to make appearances in revue and variety between April 1919 and July 1920. They worked a nine-month residency at the Hammersmith Palais, a large London ballroom. Five thousand eight hundred people paid to hear them on the opening night alone, a colossal number. The recordings and subsequent live performances of the ODJB were the starting point of a genre that shaped the sound of twentieth-century music.

This was in an era before amplification. A band playing in the enormous Hammersmith Palais ballroom worked acoustically. Asked how musicians and bands coped in full ballrooms with no amplification, ex-Jean Goldkette trombonist Spiegle Willcox (1903-1999) explained: "Vocalists used these little megaphones. Guys like Bing Crosby, Skinnay Ennis and Jack Gaylord. I remember the Mason Dixon Orchestra played a sorority house at Cornell, and the singers stood on chairs. They had to, because the sorority house was just *full* of people. By the Thirties, we had mikes." [16]

The non-segregated nature of early New Orleans music is frequently referred to by musicians of the time. "It was all mixed up there," said Wingy Manone. "Buddy Petit, Sidney Bechet, Freddie Keppard, Bunk Johnson, Nick LaRocca, the Bigards . . . we were all in one area. The musicians listened to each other, and sometimes played together in parades. They had to - there weren't enough horn players to go round. The young jazz musicians listened to everyone who came up who could play, white or colored . . . there was a mixture down there in New Orleans then. And today, black or white don't make no difference to me. I go for the truth or nothing." [17]

By contrast, at this time (1920), record companies Okeh and Vocalion began to issue Race Records. This policy, which was acceptable by the mores of the time, was soon imitated by Victor and Columbia. These were recordings made by black artists and aimed specifically at the black audience, and included a substantial amount of jazz. Race Records continued to be issued until World War II.

At first the music was called jass. Later it became jazz, and occasionally jaz. Some say that the name comes from jasmine perfume, used by prostitutes. Considering that the years of the birth of jazz were the best years of the brothels of Storyville, this is plausible. Another, again connected with sex, is that the word came from a compression of the word 'orgasm'. This became 'jasm' and then 'jass'.

Because posters could easily be defaced to render 'jass' as 'ass', advertisers took to spelling the word with 'z', as 'jaz' or 'jazz'. Some claim that the word comes from the French dialect verb, 'jaser', to chatter. Others say it is an African word meaning 'speeded up'. The effect of swing is to make the music sound as though it is pressing forward or speeding up. Jazz is also said to be slang for procreation, or sexual intercourse. There are several theories, and no way of determining which one is correct.

According to historian Dick Holbrook, the word 'jazz' seems to have been used in the San Francisco area during the late nineteenth century. The 3 March, 1906 edition of the *San Francisco Bulletin* uses the word in a sports report. The author defines jazz as somewhere between pep and enthusiasm.

Scholar and writer S. Frederick Starr offers the alternative view that the word sprang from the Old Testament *jezebel*, meaning shameless scheming woman. New Orleans usage shortened this to *jazzbo* or *jazzbeau*. Whichever way jazz was spelt, the word was in common use by 1915. [18]

Pawnshops in New Orleans were well stocked with instruments at the turn of the century. The clarinet, a member of the woodwind, has a single bamboo (or sometimes plastic) reed, which is clamped below a mouthpiece. Instruments are usually made from hardwood, mostly the very dense African blackwood, though clarinets have also been made in plastic and metal. Different notes are obtained by altering the effective length of the tube. Clarinetists do this by moving their fingers to cover and uncover the holes from which the sound emerges. Exactly the same principle is used by the penny whistle, the ocarina and the recorder.

The instruments favored by New Orleans clarinetists were the French narrow bore so-called simple system clarinets, usually with a key layout devised by the maker E. J. Albert of Brussels. The clarinet mechanism had been redesigned by the great genius of woodwind

31

instrument manufacture Theobald Boehm (1794-1881), but although the Boehm system fingering offered certain advantages, and was rapidly adopted by orchestral players, early jazz players (and later, the revivalists) remained loyal to the simple system. Interestingly, the swing era colossi of jazz clarinet playing - Benny Goodman, Artie Shaw, Buddy DeFranco, Woody Herman and Jimmy Dorsey - all played Boehm system instruments.

The main role of the clarinet in a New Orleans ensemble is to provide harmony above the trumpet and trombone. When the instruments play the same rhythms, phrasing together, it is called *homophony*. Music in strands of contrapuntal harmony is called *polyphony*. Occasionally, as in sections of the ODJB's *Livery Stable Blues*, the front line instruments (cornet, clarinet, trombone) are heard playing passages in unison, that is to say, playing exactly the same note pitches and rhythmic phrases. But mostly the clarinetist plays an answering or linking role. The clarinet can be played rapidly, and lends itself well to filling ensemble gaps by playing phrases that tail across the phrases of the cornet lead, avoiding collisions. Brass instruments (cornet, trumpet, trombone) are far louder than the clarinet. The clarinet player, required to match power in order to achieve a balanced ensemble, mostly plays above the cornet or trumpet lead.

Though in recordings made before the mid-twenties the clarinet was the reed instrument preferred by jazz musicians, saxophones are to be seen in the very first pictures of New Orleans jazz bands. They appear in early photos of the ODJB. The saxophone is categorized as a woodwind instrument, despite its brass body.

The first major jazz saxophonist was the New Orleans Creole Sidney Bechet (1897-1959), who bought a soprano saxophone when on tour in London in 1919. He was virtually the only notable soprano saxophonist in jazz throughout the first half of the century (the other was Johnny Hodges), although the New Orleans Creole clarinetist Paul Barnes claimed that *he* first introduced saxophone playing to New Orleans Jazz, "when he was seventeen going on eighteen." [19]

The role of the C-melody saxophone in early jazz must not be overlooked, though it frequently is. It is simply a tenor saxophone in C, rather than B♭, having a lighter and, of course, slightly higher sound than the tenor. Several major jazz musicians began their careers on the instrument. Benny Carter and Coleman Hawkins both began on the C-melody and, surprisingly, Paul Whiteman's pianist and arranger Bill Challis started his professional work in dance bands as a player of the C-melody. [20]

The two men to specialize on the C-melody and exert an influence on jazz history were Jack Pettis (b.1902) and, most notably, Frankie 'Tram' Trumbauer (1901-1956). Pettis, a thoughtful and agile impro-viser, is unfortunately little known today. He was the first musician to record a solo on film, in 1925; his work is worth seeking out. It was Pettis (on both tenor and C-melody) who influenced Bud Freeman. In Freeman's opinion, Pettis indirectly influenced Lester Young. But Young is also known to have had high regard for Freeman's playing. All routes point to the same sources. These two players of the C-melody were important influences on the evolution of the jazz tenor saxophone.

Of the woodwind instruments, the single reeds (clarinets and sax-ophones) predominate in jazz. Double reeds, (oboe and bassoon) are rarely encountered, though joyous performances such as *Running Ragged* and *Bamboozling the Bassoon* by Adrian Rollini, in the com-pany of Joe Venuti and Eddie Lang in the late twenties, leave one wishing for more. A later player was Illinois Jacquet (b.1922), who recorded *'Round Midnight* in 1969. Contemporary players include Paul Hanson, Ken McIntyre and Karen Borca, the latter a free jazz musician who has worked with Cecil Taylor and Andrew Cyrille.

In the New Orleans ensemble, the melody is taken by the trumpet or cornet. Both are brass instruments. The cornet's conical bore gives it a softer sound than the trumpet, though still more powerful than the other front line. In each case, trumpet and cornet, the sound is made by buzzing the lips inside a small cup-shaped mouthpiece. A combination of varying lip pressure, and altering the length of the air column with the three valves, gives different pitches of notes.

The trombone is also a brass instrument, filling in the tenor range of the harmony. There are two types of trombone, the slide trombone and the valve trombone. As with the cornet or trumpet, the sound is made by buzzing the lips inside a cup-shaped mouthpiece. Again, the different notes are obtained by a combination of varying the lip pressure and altering the length of the air column. As its name suggests, the valve trombone uses valves to route the passage of air along longer or shorter pathways. The slide version permits infinite gradations of tube length, making glissandi possible.

With this ability to sweep between notes, the slide trombone was a popular, essential member of the early New Orleans ensembles, though the valve instrument was around from the very beginning.

While the instrument was capable of great flexibility and speed, most early trombone players seemed content to regard their instrument as a musical clown. When an instrument slides from one note to the next, it is called a *glissando* (*gliss.* for short), or a *portamento*. To give the trombonist room to manipulate the slide at arm's length, bands playing outdoors on trucks or wagons placed the trombonist at the back. There they could work the slide over the tailgate, out of harm's way. New Orleans trombone quickly became known as tailgate trombone.

The trombone often follows the inner harmonic lines between the cornet or trumpet lead and the bass. These inner lines have several names. Pianists call them thumb lines. Some harmony teachers call them infra-structural lines. They are important linear strands of the chromatic harmony on which jazz is built.

Other brass instruments are relatively rare in early jazz. The exceptions are the brass basses. Both the tuba and, later, the sousaphone were used as alternatives to the string bass.

The use of mutes in jazz is almost exclusively associated with the brass instruments. Mutes are not primarily used to make instruments quiet. The name is misleading. Mutes are tone coloring devices; think of the sound as being transmuted.

The notes of a brass instrument emerge solely from the end of the bell, unlike all of the woodwind instruments where, despite an elegantly shaped bell, the sound really issues from the opened finger holes. Covering the end of the bell of a clarinet or saxophone makes a negligible difference to the tone or volume. In contrast, the effect of a trumpet or trombone can be dramatically modified if a hand is held inside, or over the end of, the bell.

It is easy to imagine how the placing of the player's free hand over the bell led to the use of a drinking glass or cup to change the timbre. This led to the development of specially designed mutes such as the straight mute, and the metal Harmon mute. Both fit snugly into the bell. Sometimes two mutes are used simultaneously, one inside the other, or a muted effect may be modified by the player's hand. The introduction of mutes for brass instruments is generally credited to the early jazz trumpet players, King Oliver in particular.

The Harmon mute consists of an aluminum cylinder, fitted with a center tube of approximately 15mm. diameter. The sound is adjusted by moving the tube in or out of the body of the mute, or removing the tube completely.

Despite the development of well-designed, handsomely finished commercially marketed mutes, many jazz players still use a rubber sink plunger, or a drinking glass. Some players are associated with a particular muted sound, for example Miles Davis with the Harmon mute, or Cootie Williams and Bubber Miley with the plunger.

Other instruments can be muted. Mutes on string instruments clamp the bridge, thus impeding the vibrations. They have been used for centuries. There is such a thing as a saxophone mute (a doughnut-shaped ring, cloth-covered, fitted inside the saxophone bell), and a device called a clarinet practicer (a box to contain the clarinet and its sound, with armholes for the player). All have subtle effects. These woodwind mutes are rarely used in musical performances.

The rhythm section is a complete band in itself. Harmonically self-sufficient, it supplies the rhythmic underpinning for the rest of the ensemble and soloists. Though usually comprised of piano, bass and drums, there are effective rhythm sections without drums, just as there are effective rhythm sections without a bass or a piano. No single instrument is an essential constituent of the rhythm section.

Rhythm section instruments are piano, string bass (bass violin, Fender bass, even tea chest bass), wind bass (sousaphone, tuba, sometimes a blown jug), drum set or trap set, other percussion including wood blocks, bones, spoons, guitar and banjo - even shuffling feet, or hand claps.

The piano was present in jazz from the beginning, not only in ragtime but also in the earliest jazz ensembles. The Original Dixieland Jazz Band had a rhythm section of piano and drums. Other bands, such as Louis Armstrong's Hot Five and Hot Seven, employed a piano in the rhythm section. Important early pianists included Jelly Roll Morton, James P. Johnson, Lil Armstrong and Earl Hines.

The guitar was heard in the earliest jazz ensembles. From the evidence of contemporary photographs, many of the New Orleans combos at the turn of the century employed a guitar in their instrumentation. Buddy Bolden's 1901 band is a good example. The commonly held notion that the banjo came first, and was supplanted by the guitar, is as inaccurate as the idea that the early bands did not use the double bass. Both the guitar and the banjo were included (separately) in the early ensembles. The banjo is louder than the acoustic guitar. After the 1920s, the banjo was heard less frequently in jazz, until the post-war Dixieland revival.

Several photos of very early jazz bands, taken in the 1890s, show one of the musicians playing a double bass. An extant photograph of John Robichaux's Orchestra, taken in New Orleans around 1893, includes a double bass - apparently with three strings. Again, Buddy Bolden's band, photographed before 1895, is seen with a double bass. It has often been said that almost all the first double bassists in jazz came from New Orleans. However, as this relatively easy instrument was played with significantly less flair than any other jazz instrument for the first decade or so of jazz history (the limitations of early recording techniques allowed bass players to avoid scrutiny; even today few listeners have a critical ear for good bass playing), it is perhaps over charitable to speak of a New Orleans *tradition* of double bass playing.

Although double basses can be used for marching bands, there is little evidence that this was done in the early New Orleans combos. The bass can be carried in a sling worn by the player. Mexican mariachi bands still use such slings for street performances. During World War II, the Glenn Miller Allied Expeditionary Forces (AEF) band accompanied marching servicemen. The rhythm section was conveyed by transporting the double bass and the drum kit on a small wheeled platform towed behind a jeep, slowly motoring along at the speed of the other marching musicians. The majority of jazz bass playing is plucked, a technique known as *pizzicato*. Playing with the bow is known as *arco*.

The drum set is also called kit percussion, drum kit or the trap set. Although used throughout today's popular music, kit percussion owes its origins to jazz. Developed from the drum combination used for marching, it was adapted to be played sitting down. The bass drum is struck by a beater actuated by a foot pedal. Two cymbals are clashed against each other by being fitted together on a vertical axis, with the lower cymbal held rigidly to a tubular post standing on the floor. The upper cymbal is clamped to a spring-loaded rod that moves up and down within the post. This rod is operated by a foot pedal. The whole mechanism is called a *hi-hat*. The side drum, or snare drum, placed on a small stand, is played with sticks, wire brushes, bamboo rods or bare hands.

Later, many other instruments were heard in jazz. Those described above were the important ones used in the first recordings, during the early part of the twentieth century.

References

1. Shapiro, N. and Hentoff, N., op. cit., p. 16.
2. Ibid.
3. Ibid., p. 21.
4. Ibid., pp.4-5.
5. Ibid., p. 90.
6. Ibid., p. 64.
7. Ibid., pp. 75-76.
8. Rust, B., 'The Original Dixieland Jazz Band, Creators of Jazz', *Jazz Journal,* Vol.54, No.12, December 2001, p.14.
9. Ibid., p. 13.
10. Jones, M., *Jazz Talking* (Da Capo Press, 2000), p.149.
11. Ibid., p. 2.
12. Rust, B., op. cit., p. 17.
13. Ibid., p. 15.
14. Nisenson, E., *Blue, The Murder of Jazz* (Da Capo, 2000), p. 50.
15. Rust, B., op. cit., p. 12.
16. Willcox, Spiegle, interviewed by Russ Tarby, published on the Internet, at: http://newtimes.rway.com/1998/042298/cover.htm
17. Jones, M., op. cit., p. 149.
18. Sudhalter, R. M., *Lost Chords* (New York: OUP, 1999), pp. 8, 9.
19. Jones, M., op. cit., p. 1.
20. Brown, J. R., *A View of the C: The Fall and Rise of the C-melody Saxophone*, IAJE Research Proceedings Yearbook, Vol. XXXI, 2001, p. 2.

3. Chicago, 1919 -1929

In 2004 there are nearly seven million people living in Chicago. This is America's third largest city; only New York and Los Angeles are bigger. The city sits in the northern center of the country, known as the Midwest.

Chicago is on the western shore of Lake Michigan. The opposite shore is beyond the horizon, about fifty miles across the water. The Lake is enormous: Israel would fit inside it. Chicago sits on the toe of the lake, at the Illinois corner, where Indiana and Wisconsin meet. Called 'the windy city,' this name is said to refer to the winds of political change, not to the weather.

Come with me to the Chicago of 1919. The Great War ended last year. Woodrow Wilson is President of the United States. Already there are nearly 110,000 motor vehicles on the city streets.[1] Some prosperous citizens own telephones. Domestic phonographs are available, but no radio. Many people have come to live in the city, mostly from the south. Prohibition, the banning of the consumption of alcohol, has begun. About this there are mixed feelings. Prohibition will remain in force across the USA until the law is repealed in 1933. Before then it will make Chicago notorious worldwide, both because of the general level of organized crime associated with Prohibition, and because of the terrible St. Valentine's Day Massacre of 1929.

That snowy February morning, five men in a police car arrived at a warehouse at 2122 North Clark Street. Three of them wore uniform, two were in civilian clothing. They entered the building. Moments later the chatter of machine-gun fire broke the stillness.

Soon after, the five drove away. A dog inside the warehouse yapped and howled. When neighbors checked, they discovered seven dead men lined up against the rear wall of the garage. They had been sprayed by machine-gun fire.

The murders, a result of inter-gang rivalry, broke the power of the North Side gang, one of several that dealt in illegal booze. The infamous Al Capone was away in Florida at the time. Nevertheless, he was behind the shooting. This was not the first Chicago gangland murder, but was extraordinary because of the effect it had on the American public.

When the equivocal Wickersham Commission Report on Prohibition was published in 1931, Franklin Pierce Adams (1881-1960) summed up the confusion in rhyme:

> Prohibition is an awful flop.
> We like it.
> It can't stop what it's meant to stop.
> We like it.
> It's left a trail of graft and slime,
> It's filled our land with vice and crime,
> It can't prohibit worth a dime,
> Nevertheless we're for it.

Chicago is popularly held to have thrived immediately after the closing of the Storyville area of New Orleans on November 12, 1917. Then, musicians were said to have 'moved up the river' to Chicago. This is confusing. It overlooks the presence of a jazz scene in Chicago before the closing of Storyville. The fact that the Mississippi flows from further north, going nowhere near Chicago, is also forgotten.

The South Side of Chicago was a racial ghetto, where the African-Americans were concentrated, the scene of hot music long before World War I. "People of both races also came to the South Side to hear clarinetist Wilbur Sweatman, a vaudeville/novelty instrumentalist who presented mixed programs of classical music, gypsy airs, and hot syncopated numbers to Chicagoans as early as 1906. Sweatman was famous for his [trick of] playing [a tune of the day], *The Rosary,* on three clarinets simultaneously, and in harmony... Sweatman's clarinet style was so unprecedented in Chicago that even musically sophisticated black listeners found it strange. He was such a hit with his queer style of playing hot clarinet that Broadway subsequently went wild about him. People of both races came to hear this three-piece orchestra play. They didn't yet call it jazz; they called it 'hot music'. Sweatman later claimed to have recorded the first jazz records ever made, in 1912 for Columbia Records, and advertised himself as 'Originator and Much Imitated Ragtime and Jazz Clarionetist'. " [2]

In May 1915 a white band (also a five-piece) from New Orleans opened in Chicago. Advertised as 'Brown's Band from Dixieland,' under the leadership of trombonist Tom Brown, the personnel included New Orleans clarinetist Larry Shields, soon to join the ODJB. They played for dancing, used the words 'ragtime' and 'jass' in their publicity, and their repertoire included *Memphis Blues* and *Livery Stable Blues.* Their four month engagement was at Lamb's Cafe, at the intersection of North Clark and Randolph streets. [3] This band had a sound very similar to that of the ODJB.

Thus, jazz was heard in Chicago before the great migration years, 1916 to 1919. Jelly Roll Morton's band was playing in the South Side cabarets in 1914 and 1915. "The word 'jass' first appeared in the city's black press... on September 30, 1916, when the Chicago *Defender* used the word to describe music produced by black pianist-songwriter

W. Benton Overstreet in support of vaudevillian Estella Harris at the Grand Theater. Harris, variously labeled as a 'Coon Shouter' and 'Rag Shouter,' was now accompanied by a 'Jass Band'.... Very soon thereafter, a variant spelling of the term - 'Jaz' - was used in the Indianapolis Freeman to describe an instrumental group." [4]

Approximately half a million blacks from the southern states moved north to Chicago during the great migration of 1916-1919, and another one million followed during the 1920s. The arrival of so many folk from Louisiana, Mississippi, Alabama, Arkansas and Texas stimulated the jazz age in Chicago. Most of the South Side's jazz musicians arrived at the height of this migration. For example, bassist Bill Johnson, cornetist Freddie Keppard, pianist Lil Hardin and reed player Sidney Bechet all arrived in 1918. [5]

The *Jazz Age* was the name F. Scott Fitzgerald gave to the 1920s, the *Roaring Twenties*. Those postwar years saw numerous changes. Although there had been no fighting on home soil, many Americans were disillusioned by the shocking experiences of the war. A decreasing interest in world affairs ensued. Anti-foreign sentiment enabled the rise of the racist, anti-Semitic and anti-Catholic Ku Klux Klan. Originating near Atlanta in 1915, it was the second of two secret organizations of that name. Previously, a similar organization had arisen after the Civil War. That had lasted until the 1870s.

Racist lynchings in the South were the result of these new Klan activities. Sixty-four lynchings occurred in 1918, eighty-three in 1919. Race riots broke out in several cities. The worst was in the South Side district of Chicago in 1919. For thirteen days the city was without law and order. Thirty-eight people died, twenty-three blacks and fifteen whites. This was a low point, for the riots shocked the American nation out of indifference towards racial tension and conflict.

There were other regressive moves after the war. Rural areas, particularly in the South, saw a rise in the strength of a Christian fundamentalist movement. This aided the introduction of Prohibition. A law was passed in the Southern States which banned the teaching of evolution!

Now there was increasing prosperity. Mass production and industrialization increased the comfort of the ordinary person's life, with more money earned for fewer hours worked. In these postwar years, air travel developed. Ownership of a motor car, domestic refrigerator and telephone became common. Tabloid newspapers, magazines, radio and the cinema prospered. During the war, women had gone out to work. Employed in industry, they often did jobs formerly done by men. Understandably, women were unwilling to relinquish their new social and economic independence. This led to further emancipation of women after the war.

Women's suffrage, the right to vote in national and local elections, had been an issue throughout the nineteenth century. Women had secured the vote in New Zealand in 1893, in Australia in 1902, in Finland 1906 and in Norway in 1913. World War I had speeded up the enfranchisement of women in many countries of the world, and women were given the vote in America in 1920. Now they wore their hair and skirts shorter. They smoked and drank in public, abandoned their corsets and felt free to express opinions of their own. They even discussed sex more openly.

For both men and women, the world of jazz - with its vigorous dancing, flappers with bobbed hair, speakeasies offering illegal booze and the proximity of bootleggers - was exciting. Jazz could be vicariously relished through the new media of picture magazines, radio and the movies.

In jazz, Louis Armstrong (his name sometimes pronounced 'Lewis') dominates this decade. Louis was born in New Orleans on 4 August, 1901. His grandparents had been slaves, and his father left his mother as soon as Louis was born. His mother became a prostitute. He was raised in poverty, in a two-roomed house with an outside lavatory. Louis Armstrong (or *Satch, Satchelmouth, Reverend Satchelmouth, Pops, Gate, King Louis* - he had multiple titles) died on 6 July, 1971. He is the great genius whose virtuosity and invention transformed jazz.

Louis was also blessed with an ingenuous nature, possessing an almost unparalleled ability to make people smile. Long after his death it is a pleasure to share video recordings of Louis with today's jazz history students. To see teenage faces light up at Louis's comments, his jokes, his beaming smile and his thrilling, coherent playing, is wonderful. Miles Davis once said, "You can't play nothing on trumpet that doesn't come from him, not even modern shit." [6] That goes for all instruments, and jazz of all eras.

Genesis and genius generate conjecture, never more so than with Louis. Where did he find his melodic and harmonic ideas? From the very beginning of his recorded output, he displays blinding musical *aperçus*, far more dazzling than those of his contemporaries. No wonder some enthusiasts deify him, regarding him as being suffused with an aura of the divine.

Louis grew up in New Orleans. From 1913, he lived in the Home for Colored Waifs, placed there as a result of firing a pistol into the air on New Year's Day. This punishment was to transfigure jazz. At the home, Louis was given the opportunity to learn the cornet. He took part in a brass band. Later in life Louis claimed that as a child he was influenced by Bunk Johnson, but Louis's main inspiration and teacher was King Oliver, who played in the band led by trombonist Kid Ory.

After 1917, when the infamous Storyville area in New Orleans was closed, and many musicians relocated to Chicago, King Oliver was one of those who made the journey north. In New Orleans, Louis took over King Oliver's job in the Kid Ory band. Of Louis at that time, Kid Ory said, "He had a wonderful ear and a wonderful memory. All you had to do was to hum or whistle a new tune to him and he'd know it right away. And if he played a tune once, he never forgot it. Within six months, everybody in New Orleans knew about him." [7]

In 1919 Louis joined the Kentucky Jazz Band of pianist Fate Marable (1890-1947).This band, which worked out of St. Louis, played on the Mississippi steamboats. At various times some of the best jazz musicians worked in the Marable band. They included drummer Baby Dodds and banjoist Johnny St Cyr.

Then, in 1922, Louis moved north to Chicago to join King Oliver's Creole Jazz Band at the Lincoln Gardens. This meant that Oliver added a second cornet to the standard New Orleans front line instrumentation of cornet, clarinet and trombone. Louis had to adapt to this, to find an extra strand to play in the improvised polyphony. He accomplished this difficult task brilliantly.

You can hear Oliver and Armstrong together in *Mabel's Dream*, and two recordings of *Dippermouth Blues*, recorded in 1923. Immediately, these were highly regarded by other musicians. *Dippermouth* was another affectionate reference to the size of Louis's mouth, 'as large as a dipper'.

By 1924, Louis had quit Oliver's band. He left Chicago for New York, where he joined the band of Fletcher Henderson - at the time the top New York band - for one year. He also recorded with Bessie Smith, their five sides including *St. Louis Blues*. A collaboration with Sidney

Bechet produced an impressive *Cake-Walking Babies from Home*. In 1925, Louis Armstrong returned to Chicago. In the following years, particularly in 1927 and 1928, he made several outstanding recordings that set the style for the ensuing Swing Era. They have continued to delight and impress listeners ever since.

The Hot Five and Hot Seven began their series of recordings in November, 1925. The musicians with Armstrong included Edward 'Kid' Ory on trombone, and Johnny Dodds on clarinet, pianist Lil Armstrong (replaced on some sides by Earl Hines), and banjoist Johnny St Cyr. For the Hot Seven recordings this quintet was joined by Pete Briggs on tuba and Baby Dodds on drums. Outstanding sides include *Cornet Chop Suey* (1926), *Potato Head Blues* (1927) (wherein Louis's solo is magical), and *West End Blues* (1928). *West End Blues*, with Earl Hines, opens with an unaccompanied trumpet cadenza that was ground-breaking at the time. Louis's solo has been imitated or paraphrased in every decade since.

"We made our first records in Chicago at the Okeh studios, and, of course, when we made them we didn't have any expectation that they would be as successful as they became," said Kid Ory. "One thing that helped the sale was the fact that for a while the Okeh people gave away a picture of Louis to everyone that bought one of the records. When they did that, the sales went way up, because Louis was so popular." [8]

In the same year Louis and Earl Hines recorded the outstanding, most significant, jazz side of the decade, *Weather Bird Rag*. This is a delightful duet improvisation that has Armstrong and Hines, both still in their twenties, challenging each other and taking chances in a tension-building performance of great virtuosity.

The Hot Fives and Hot Sevens represent an abundant thesaurus of jazz devices. Louis's contribution includes scat singing, which is the technique of singing improvised nonsense syllables. Louis is credited with inventing this technique out of necessity when he dropped his music during a rehearsal and could not remember the words. Certainly he makes the scat technique all his own on *Heebie Jeebies* (1926) and *Hotter Than That* (1927).

Jelly Roll Morton claimed that he had invented scat, but after these performances its first appearance has always been associated with Louis. "*Heebie Jeebies* was what today would be called a hit record. That was the record where Louis forgot the lyrics and started scattin'! We had all we could do to keep from laughing. Of course, Louis said he forgot the words, but I don't know if he intended it that way or not. It made the record, though." [9] Others have since observed that Louis was singing like this when on the streets of New Orleans as a child, long before the record appeared.

During all of the subsequent changes in jazz, through all of the various fashions and styles, Louis Armstrong continued to work. He appeared in movies and on television, toured the world with his band, the All Stars, and still made records. In 1967, towards the end of his life, Louis made a recording of *What a Wonderful World*, singing in his gentle, gravelly voice. Popular first in Britain, it has enjoyed periodic revivals. The recording became established in the United States when it was featured in the movie *Good Morning, Vietnam*, twenty years later.

For today's youthful listener, if Louis Armstrong's name is known at all it is because of this song. Ironic, then, that the first great genius of jazz, the man who set the style for jazz trumpet, who invented scat singing, is now best remembered for singing a sentimental popular song. In 2001 the city of New Orleans renamed its airport as Louis Armstrong International Airport.

What Were Louis Armstrong's Achievements?

• His influence can be heard in almost all the important jazz players prominent before the coming of bebop in the 1940s - and not just trumpeters.

• He was one of the first great soloists in jazz history, having a wider range and better command of the trumpet than any of his contemporaries.

• He led the move away from group improvisation to solo improvisation.

• Whilst not the only player to eschew the 'melodic paraphrase' approach to improvising, and to improvise on the chord progression, he was the most prominent soloist to do this.

• He had a developed sense of drama and pacing, with a sure touch in bringing about a climactic ending, and the ability to create solos replete with surprise and tension.

• He popularized scat singing.

The first jazz to be recorded was played by New Orleans musicians who had moved to Chicago, chief among them being the ODJB, Louis Armstrong, King Oliver, Sidney Bechet, Jelly Roll Morton, Kid Ory and the New Orleans Rhythm Kings (NORK). All the early New

Orleans jazz recordings were made in Chicago. One can reasonably assume that by the time the musicians had become established in Chicago, their music had changed.

Thus, two styles of jazz evolved in Chicago simultaneously. One style was represented by the musicians who had moved up from New Orleans. The other was produced by a group of younger musicians, mostly white Chicagoans. They played what became known as Chicago Jazz, or the Chicago School.

Several of these young white musicians attended the same school in the city, Austin High. In prose that could have been written by Damon Runyon, Mezz Mezzrow described the well-to-do Chicago suburb of Austin. "All the days were Sabbaths, a sleepy-time neighborhood big as a yawn and just about as lively, loaded with shade-trees and clipped lawns and a groggy-eyed population that never came out of its coma except to turn over."[10] The Austin High musicians included cornetist Jimmy McPartland, clarinetist Frank Teschemacher (1906-1932) and tenor saxophonist Bud Freeman.

Jimmy McPartland described how he had become interested in jazz: "Every day after school, Frank Teschemacher and Bud Freeman, Jim Lanigan, my brother Dick, myself, and a few others used to go to a little place called the Spoon and Straw. It was just an ice-cream parlor where you'd get a malted milk, soda, shakes and all that stuff... One day they had some new Gennett records on the table, and we put them on. They were by the New Orleans Rhythm Kings, and I believe the first tune we played was *Farewell Blues*. Boy, when we heard this - I'll tell you, we went out of our minds... We stayed there from about three in the afternoon until eight at night, just listening to those records one after another, over and over again. Right then and there we decided we would get a band and try to play like these guys." [11]

Other young Chicagoans included drummers Ben Pollack, Dave Tough and Gene Krupa, clarinetists Benny Goodman and Mezz Mezzrow, guitarist Eddie Condon and pianist Joe Sullivan. The city was regarded as an exciting place. "Eddie Condon later claimed that in 1924-26, at the height of the jazz age, a trumpet held up in the night air of the Stroll would play itself. Stores remained open twenty-four hours a day to serve those enjoying urban life after years of rural tranquility. During the day, women wearing what the *Defender* called 'head rags of gaudy hues' leaned from tenement windows, while small groups of men asserted a more public presence on the sidewalks. At night the crowded sidewalks rang with music and laughter. Langston Hughes, visiting from New York in 1918, recalled that 'midnight was like day.' " [12] Hot venues in the city included the Savoy Ballroom, the Royal Gardens, the Apex Club, the Sunset Café, and the two most famous, the Dreamland Café, which opened in 1914 'with 125 electric lights', [13] and the Grand Terrace, which opened in 1928. Chicago was the jazz center of the world during the 1920s. "All the young musicians in town would come to hear Louis - Benny Goodman, Muggsy Spanier and the rest," said impresario Joe Glaser, "I used to let them in free. Hell, they were kids, and never had any money." [14]

Bix Beiderbecke (1903-1931) was born in Davenport, Iowa, on the Mississippi. The river boats cruising up from New Orleans visited Davenport. Bix heard Louis Armstrong when a paddle steamer on which Armstrong was working called at the town.

Bix learned piano as a child. At the age of two he played standing at the keyboard, reaching with his hands over his head. He had made sufficient advance at the age of seven to be featured in the *Davenport Daily Democrat*. His sister recalled that even as a very young child, Bix played his piano assignments 'with improvements', that is, with improvised embellishments. [15] Cornet playing came later. His style was modeled on that of the ODJB's Nick LaRocca, whom he copied by listening to gramophone recordings. Of course, Bix studied Louis Armstrong's records after Louis began recording in 1923.

Bix completed his education at a school near Chicago. He spent time in the city, though his playing does not fit neatly into the category of Chicago style. On both piano and cornet he exhibited a brilliant ability to hear harmonies and play by ear, but was never a fluent reader of music. Bix's piano composition *In a Mist* gives a good indication of his fondness for impressionistic harmonies, with its opening descending chords containing ninths, sharpened elevenths and thirteenths.

"Bix had a miraculous ear," observed Pee Wee Russell. "As for classical music, Bix liked little things like some of those compositions of MacDowell and Debussy - very light things. Delius, for example. Then he made a big jump from that sort of thing to Stravinsky and stuff like that. There'd be certain things he would hear in some modern classical music, like whole tones, and he'd say, why not do it in a jazz band? What's the difference? Music doesn't have to be the sort of thing that's put in brackets? Then later it got to be like a fad and everybody did it, but they wouldn't know what the devil it was all about." [16]

Bix also enjoyed the orchestral music of Ravel, and the American composer Eastwood Lane, a musician who goes unmentioned in many reference books.

"Louis Armstrong was Bix Beiderbecke's idol," said Hoagy Carmichael, who first heard Bix with the Wolverines. "I learned that Bix was no imitation of Armstrong. The Wolverines sounded better to me than the New Orleans Rhythm Kings. Theirs was a stronger rhythm, and the licks that Jimmy Hartwell, George Johnson and Bix played were precise and beautiful. Bix's breaks were not as wild as Armstrong's, but they were hot, and he selected each note with musical care. He showed me that jazz could be musical and beautiful as well as hot. He showed me that tempo doesn't mean fast. His music affected me in a different way. Can't tell you how - like licorice, you have to eat some." [17]

Bix's first recordings were made in 1924, with a small group known as the Wolverines Orchestra, modeled on the New Orleans Rhythm Kings (NORK). In 1926, Bix recorded with pianist Jean Goldkette's Orchestra in Detroit. He moved to the orchestra of Paul Whiteman from 1927 to 1930. The Whiteman career began during World War I, when he led a forty-piece navy orchestra.

In 1920 Whiteman sold a million copies of a recording of *Whispering*. His orchestra functioned as a popular touring concert orchestra playing jazzy arrangements of current songs and light classics. Enjoying a long, successful existence, the band toured Britain in 1923, Europe in 1926. Whiteman continued prominently in music until the 1950s. High spots of his career included an Aeolian Hall, New York concert in 1924, when George Gershwin (1898-1937) premiered his own *Rhapsody in Blue*. The Whiteman band appeared in a string of films, beginning with the *King of Jazz* in 1930, a title resented by many jazz musicians, for the orchestra was *not* a forerunner of the later swing bands. However, history has been unfairly dismissive of the achievements of Whiteman. We should remember that Whiteman was a key figure in American popular music, occasionally giving employment to Bix, saxophonist Frank Trumbauer, guitarist Eddie Lang and others.

Away from Whiteman, Bix Beiderbecke is heard at his magical best in recordings such as *I'm Coming Virginia* and *Singin' the Blues* (1927). In the latter, Bix is matched to perfection by C-melody saxophonist Frank Trumbauer.

Adrian Rollini's bass saxophone playing is also outstanding. He was alone in defining a role for the instrument. "His modern conception and well-constructed continuity, anticipates the work of modern jazz musicians like Gerry Mulligan and Pepper Adams by some twenty years," wrote Gunther Schuller. [18]

Bix had an immense effect on everyone around him, well summed up by guitarist Eddie Condon's account of first hearing Bix play. "All my life I had been listening to music, particularly on the piano. But I had never heard anything remotely resembling what Beiderbecke played," he said. "For the first time I realized that music isn't all the same, that some people play so differently from others that it becomes an entirely new set of sounds. That was the first time I heard the New Orleans Rhythm Kings, except on records, but I actually didn't hear them at all; I listened to Beiderbecke. When we rushed out to grab our train I was completely confused. Trying to get to sleep in an upper berth I kept thinking - what about the cornet, can he play that too?"

Condon found out the next day. "With nothing to do but sit and stare at the scenery from Cleveland to Buffalo, I began to wonder again about the cornet. I got out my banjo. Eberhardt dug up his saxophone and doodled along with me. Finally Beiderbecke took out a silver cornet. He put it to his lips and blew a phrase. The sound came out like a girl saying yes." [19]

The enforced ban on the sale of alcohol, introduced at the time of the postwar great migration, was called Prohibition. It was not solely a North American idea. Even today, some Muslim countries ban alcohol.

Attempts at Prohibition have been made in Iceland, Norway, Sweden, Russia, Canada and India. In the United States, movements towards Prohibition began in the nineteenth century, alongside movements towards the abolition of slavery.

The first American Prohibition laws were passed in Maine in 1846, beginning a wave of such legislation before the Civil War. But now came Prohibition on a national scale. In October 1919 the National Prohibition Act, known as the Volstead Act (after its promoter Congressman Andrew J. Volstead), was passed, giving enforcement guidelines. Interestingly, Finland adopted Prohibition in the same year.

In the United States, Prohibition began at midnight on 16 January, 1920. Enforcement of the law was patchy, depending largely on the local attitude. The tolerance in towns and cities was considerable, the implementation of the law weak. Prohibition poured customers into the places where jazz was played. Millions of otherwise law-abiding citizens drank prohibited liquor, thus contributing to organized crime. With Prohibition, the price of drink increased. Bootlegging (the brewing, distribution and sale of illegal liquor), developed on a large scale. The speakeasy, an illegal drinking den, flourished. This was often a place of employment for jazz musicians.

Of the gang leaders who prospered as a result of Prohibition, Al Capone was the most notorious, largely because of the infamous St Valentine's Day Massacre (see page 40). One authority put Capone's annual earnings from bootleg alcohol alone in 1929 at an incredible $60,000,000. [20] Eventually he spent six and a half years in Alcatraz prison on tax evasion charges, dying at the age of 48.

In time, even the supporters of Prohibition saw that the legislation did not work, and became disenchanted . ith the idea. With the coming of the Great Depression, alcohol ceased to be a key political issue. By 1933 Prohibition was repealed. Drinking alcohol was legal again, but only in some states.

Amazingly, it took until 1966 for all states to change the legislation.

References

1. Platt, H.L., Loyola University of Chicago, website http://www.lib.uchicago.edu/
2. Kenney, W. H., *Chicago Jazz* (OUP, 1993), p. 8.
3. Ibid., p. 67.
4. Ibid., p. 11.
5. Ibid., p. 12.
6. Davis, M. and Troupe, Q., *Miles: The Autobiography* (Simon and Schuster, 1989), p. 316.
7. Shapiro, N. and Hentoff, N., op. cit., p. 61.
8. Ibid., p. 109.
9. Ibid.
10. Mezzrow, M. and Wolfe, B., *Really the Blues* (London: Corgi Books, 1961), p. 109.
11. Shapiro, N. and Hentoff, N., op. cit., pp. 118-119.
12. Kenney, W. H., op. cit., p. 15.
13. Ibid., p. 18.
14. Shapiro, N. and Hentoff, N., op. cit., p. 115.
15. Bridget Berman documentary film about Bix's life.
16. Shapiro, N. and Hentoff, N., op. cit., p. 155.
17. Ibid., p. 142.
18. Schuller, G., *Early Jazz: Its Roots and Musical Development* (OUP, 1968), p. 255, note 7.

19.   Condon, E., *We Called It Music* (London: Corgi Books, 1962), p. 56.

20.   *Encyclopedia Britannica* (Chicago: Encyclopedia Britannica Inc., 2003).

4. New York, New York
Cotton Club to Carnegie Hall

Harlem is the area north of Central Park in Manhattan, New York, lying between 110th Street, the East River, Harlem River and 168th Street. By the turn of the century, Harlem had a large Jewish population. After 1910 it was the scene of increasing African-American migration from the South. Soon it became the largest and most influential African-American community in North America, one of the centers of innovation in jazz.

By 1920, as a result of the migration north, 200,000 blacks lived there. The area teemed with jazz activity during the period between the two World Wars, a period now known as the Harlem Renaissance. Much of everyday Harlem life during that era has entered jazz history. Harlem was home to the singer Ella Fitzgerald, bandleader Duke Ellington, writer Langston Hughes, politicians Adam Clayton Powell, Jr. and Malcolm X.

Harlem gave its name to a style of piano playing, Harlem Stride. Harlem rent parties were famous, when money to pay the rent was raised by hiring a stride pianist, then organizing a house party where the guests were charged a small amount of money to help pay the rent. One writer described Harlem as 'The New Storyville'. Even the best known photograph in jazz, 'The Big Picture' or 'The Great Jazz Day', taken in 1958 for *Esquire* magazine's 'Golden Age of Jazz' issue, published in 1959 and containing 57 of the greatest jazz faces, was posed against the backdrop of a Harlem brownstone house, number 17, at 126th Street between Madison and Fifth Avenues.

Today one still takes the 'A' Train to get to Harlem. Its name is celebrated in such titles as *Drop Me Off In Harlem*, *Harlem Nocturne* and Ellington's *Harlem Air Shaft*. From the 1920s onwards there were dozens of clubs and ballrooms between 125th and 135th Streets. They included the Apollo Theater, 253 West 125th Street; Connie's Inn, 2221 Adam Clayton Powell Boulevard; Harlem Opera House, 211 West 125th Street; Minton's Playhouse, 210 West 118th Street; (Clarke) Monroe's Uptown House, 2259 Seventh Avenue; Pod and Jerry's, 166 West 133rd Street; Savoy Ballroom at 596 Lenox Avenue; Small's Paradise, 2294 Seventh Avenue - and the Cotton Club.

The Cotton Club was the most famous. Opened in 1920 at 644 Lenox Avenue as the Club Deluxe, it changed its name to the Cotton Club in 1922, attracting a largely white clientele until 1935, the year of the Harlem race riots. After that, the area was considered unsafe for the whites who constituted the club's customers. From 1936 until 1940 the Cotton Club moved downtown, away from Harlem at 200 West 48th Street.

Bands that appeared at the Cotton Club included those of Cab Calloway, Duke Ellington, and Jimmie Lunceford. Individuals such as Louis Armstrong, singers Ivie Anderson and Ethel Waters, and dancers Bill Robinson and the Nicholas Brothers appeared there. Harlem also played its part in the early bop experiments. Thelonious Monk was a member of the house band at Minton's Playhouse from 1940 to 1943, an important bop incubator. In 1984, Francis Ford Coppola's film *The Cotton Club* recreated the heyday of the club.

The Rise of the Big Band

Of course, there was jazz activity downtown. Before the 1920s, New York had witnessed the new jazz sounds coming in from New Orleans and Chicago. As early as 1917, at the very start of the era of recorded jazz, the Original Dixieland Jazz Band had appeared in New York, at Reisenweber's Restaurant, on Eighth Avenue near Columbus Circle. Duke Ellington's band was at the Kentucky Club (formerly the Hollywood) on Broadway in 1923, moving to the Cotton Club for a four-year stay from 1927.

Earlier, in 1924, Fletcher Henderson's band performed at the Club Alabam. In that year Fletcher Henderson brought Louis Armstrong to New York. Intermittently, from 1924 until 1930, Henderson had a band at the famous Roseland Ballroom on Broadway at Times Square. The Roseland had opened in 1919. Jean Goldkette's band, with Bix Beiderbecke, was at the Roseland from 1926 until 1931. Subsequently the Roseland hosted most of the major bands of the time, including McKinney's Cotton Pickers, the Casa Loma Orchestra, Claude Hopkins, Andy Kirk, Chick Webb, Luis Russell, Count Basie, and Benny Carter.

Large ensembles had existed on the fringes of jazz from the very beginning. The early New Orleans bands performing on the shores of Lake Pontchartrain at the turn of the century were akin to military bands or marching bands, playing rhythmic popular music of the day. They played from written music, using standard published scores (known as stock orchestrations), with no improvisation.

The band of James Reese Europe (1880-1919), The Hellfighters, that toured Britain and France and entered Germany towards the end of World War I, was a large ensemble that played rags and other rhythmic music to entertain the troops. In 1912, Europe had led 125 musicians in a performance called 'Concert of Negro Music', in Carnegie Hall. On his return to the USA he continued to tour, until murdered by a knife wound to the neck in Boston in May, 1919. [1]

Will Marion Cook (1869-1944), an important composer for the black musical theater, led several bands in New York between 1900 and 1920. He toured and visited England with the Southern Syncopated Orchestra between 1918 and 1920. The instrumentation was described in 1919 by Ernest Ansermet as: "Two violins, a cello, a saxophone, two basses, two clarinets, a horn, three trumpets, three trombones, drums, two pianos and a banjo section." [2]

Now there was scope for improvisation. Ansermet, the prestigious conductor friend of Igor Stravinsky, who gave the world premieres of *Histoire du soldat*, *Chant du rossignol* and *Pulcinella*, had great praise for the young Sidney Bechet: "There is in the Southern Syncopated Orchestra an extraordinary clarinet virtuoso who is, so it seems, the first of his race to have composed perfectly formed blues on the clarinet. I've heard two of them which he elaborated at great length. They are admirable equally for their richness of invention, their force of accent, and their daring novelty and unexpected turns. These solos already show the germ of a new style. Their form is gripping, abrupt, harsh, with a brusque and pitiless ending like that of Bach's Second Brandenburg Concerto. I wish to set down the name of this artist of genius; as for myself, I shall never forget it - it is Sidney Bechet." [3]

The evolution of the larger jazz ensemble was complicated, a process of expanding jazz instrumentation and developing jazz ensemble techniques, from Jelly Roll Morton via Fletcher Henderson, Don Redman, Luis Russell and Duke Ellington, as they move away from the traditional trumpet-clarinet-trombone front line of early New Orleans polyphony, adding extra instruments, using denser harmony and exploring various arranging devices.

The first important jazz composer and arranger was Jelly Roll Morton. He stands at the beginning of the process of developing a larger jazz ensemble from the simple three front line of the New Orleans jazz band. Morton planned his pieces carefully, and paid attention to form, thematic variety, and organic unity. "I'll tell you how he was in rehearsing a band," said clarinetist Omer Simeon. "He was exact with us. Very jolly, very full of life all the time, but serious. We used to spend maybe three hours rehearsing four sides, and in that time he'd give us the effects he wanted, like the background behind a solo - he would run that over on the piano with one finger and the guys would get together and harmonize it." [4]

Yet behind this there were already large ensembles in existence. Here the Paul Whiteman Orchestra deserves a mention. Whiteman led an ensemble of nineteen or twenty players, and up to seven strings.[5] He famously employed Bix Beiderbecke. Paul Whiteman has been largely dismissed by the critics. An exception is Gunther Schuller, who summarizes matters fairly: "But often enough - to make the point worth making - the arrangements were marvels of orchestrational ingenuity. They were designed to make people listen to music, not to dance. The arrangers made full use of the coloristic variety of Whiteman's basic instrumentation of nineteen or twenty players, augmented by from four to seven strings. The reedmen, particularly the great Chester Hazlett (who played the clarinet solo in the first performance of Gershwin's *Rhapsody in Blue* in the 1924 Aeolian Hall concert), Frank Trumbauer and Charles Strickfadden were all superb doublers on different instruments. The resultant performances were often more than merely slick. Excellent intonation, perfect balances, and clean attacks do not necessarily equate with superficiality. There is in the best Whiteman performances a feeling and a personal sound as unique in its way as Ellington's or Basie's. It was just not based on a jazz conception." [6]

The arranger responsible for shaping much of the sound of the Whiteman band, for pioneering the saxes and brass ensemble from which the big band era grew, was Bill Challis. In the words of Gene Lees, Challis was "one of the most overlooked and underestimated men in jazz history." [7]

The instrumentation of the big band in jazz evolved during the late twenties and early thirties, with various numbers of brass, saxophones and a three or four piece rhythm section. Saxophone sections went from three to four and eventually to five players. Trumpets went from two players to three, then eventually to four and even five. Trombones grew from one player to two, then to three. Bass trombones, along with baritone saxophones, were relatively late additions to the instrumentation.

The future of the big band lay in New York, where the center of the music industry was based - music publishing, recording, broadcasting, theater circuits and clubs. Fletcher Henderson (1897-1952) moved to New York in 1920. Along with Luis Russell (1902-1963), Henderson is one of the pioneers of the big band. Don Redman (1900-1964) became his arranger. Together, he and Henderson developed a means of organizing a jazz ensemble of between nine and twelve musicians.

In 1924, the Henderson band moved to the Roseland Ballroom in New York, and that same year Louis Armstrong joined the band. Other Henderson musicians included saxophonist Coleman Hawkins and clarinetist Buster Bailey. Benny Carter (1907-2003) joined as arranger, writing for the band from during the late twenties and early thirties. The instrumentation was five brass, three reeds, four rhythm.

Typical for the period was the band that Benny Goodman employed for his epoch-making Carnegie Hall Jazz Concert in January, 1938. Goodman used thirteen musicians - three trumpets, two trombones, four saxophones and a four-piece rhythm section. Benny added his clarinet to this instrumentation, but he was used by the arrangers mainly as a soloist, not as part of the texture. By then, Benny had begun to hire Fletcher Henderson to write arrangements for the band.

Ever since, the big band instrumentation has relentlessly increased in size. But there were extra developments besides merely adding instruments. Call and answer (antiphony), riffs, counterpoint between sections, and many more imaginative techniques, were utilized.

Other influential bands of the thirties were those of Count Basie, the Dorsey Brothers (Tommy and Jimmy), Duke Ellington, Jimmie Lunceford, Jay McShann, Artie Shaw, and Chick Webb.

In piano bars, jam sessions and rent parties, pianists such as Luckey Roberts, Willie 'The Lion' Smith and James P. Johnson developed the style known as stride piano. They laid the foundation for the next generation of pianists, which included Earl Hines and Fats Waller.

The glory of stride piano lies in the variety of pianistic techniques used to drive the music forward, to 'keep the motor going'. Although a left-hand pattern of a bass note on beats one and three, and a chord on beats two and four is one of the techniques used, there is a rich variety of further patterns and devices.

In 1943, Harlem was the scene of violent events connected with race conflicts that had begun earlier in Los Angeles, known as the Zoot Suit Riots.

The Savoy Ballroom was closed by the military. The official reason given was that servicemen had contracted venereal disease there. Those in Harlem knew the real reason was because different races mingled at the dance hall. Some suggested that its closure was a first step towards the segregation of the city. When the Zoot Suit Riots broke out, they spread to Harlem as race war. Businesses were broken into and destroyed. Cars were overturned. People were beaten and six were killed. Where once you could see many established Harlem residents financially well-off, the area started to become a center of poverty. For a long period it was regarded by whites as a dangerous place to visit.

Influential Soloists of the Thirties

Joe Venuti and Eddie Lang

Joe Venuti (1903-1978) was the first important violinist of jazz. The series of outstanding violin and guitar duo performances he made between 1926 and 1928 with Eddie Lang (1902-1933), the first great jazz guitar virtuoso, was a major influence on the playing of Django Reinhardt and Stephane Grappelli.

Venuti was said to have been born on a ship traveling from Italy to America. He was ten years old when he arrived in America; it must have been a very slow ship. Why his age was obscured is not known. He and Lang grew up as friends in Philadelphia. They played and recorded together from 1913, until Lang's premature death in 1933 from a poorly executed tonsillectomy. Venuti lived until 1978.

Initially, Joe Venuti trained to be a classical violinist. Eddie Lang also studied the violin for eleven years before switching to guitar. As colleagues they played with many of the leading jazz musicians of the time, including Jimmy Dorsey, Benny Goodman, Red Nichols, Frank Signorelli, Jack Teagarden and Frankie Trumbauer.

Lang was versatile. He could back blues singers, play classical music and be at ease performing with the greatest musicians of his day. He worked regularly with Bing Crosby during the early 1930s, appearing briefly with him in the film *The Big Broadcast*. The three of them, Venuti, Lang and Crosby, were together in Paul Whiteman's band. Bing was deeply upset by Lang's death because he had urged Lang to have the operation that ended his life.

Art Tatum

Born in the same year as Lester Young, Art Tatum (1909-1956) had a similarly short life. One of the most admired pianists in jazz history, Tatum's technical mastery, Lisztian in its supremacy, caused some listeners to be convinced that they were hearing two pianists rather than one. As a teenager, André Previn was so taken by Tatum's virtuosity that he took the trouble to transcribe some of the older man's recorded performances in order to study exactly what Tatum was doing.

Hear Tatum's recording of *Tiger Rag*, or his version of Dvorak's *Humoresque*. Tatum stands at a crossroads between swing and bebop, with a formidable, unmatchable command of the stride style. Much of his work was as an unaccompanied soloist. He is heard to best advantage when unfettered by others. Tatum had an impressive ability to incorporate additional chords as he played. Importantly, his harmonic innovations were picked up by Charlie Parker and others in the subsequent bop revolution. Parker had taken a job washing dishes in the restaurant where Tatum was playing, so that he could hear the pianist.

Fats Waller also idolized Art Tatum. "Once, when Tatum entered a club where Fats was performing, he stopped the music and announced: 'Ladies and Gentlemen, I play piano, but God is in the house tonight!'" wrote Dan Morgenstern in a liner note. "Tatum was a sort of deity to his fellow musicians - not just to pianists, but players of any instrument. No practitioner of the music called jazz had (or has) such perfect technical command, in the traditional sense, as did Art Tatum. But it was not just his astonishing facility that inspired awe in his colleagues. It was his phenomenal harmonic sense, his equally uncanny rhythmic gift, and his boundless imagination. Technique was merely the vehicle through which he expressed himself. What others could imagine, Tatum could execute, and what he could imagine went beyond the wildest dreams of mere musical mortals." [8]

Charlie Christian

In his tragically short life Charlie Christian (1916-1942) introduced the amplified hollow-bodied electric guitar to jazz. In only two years of prominent professional work he changed the role of the guitar as a jazz instrument. Hear his *Solo Flight* with the Benny Goodman band to appreciate his long single-note lines. His smoothly swinging eighth-note improvisations were influenced by his saxophone peers rather than fellow guitarists. There are amateur recordings of him with Thelonious Monk and Dizzy Gillespie; had he lived he would have made a major contribution to bebop.

Jimmy Blanton

In common with Charlie Christian, bassist Jimmy Blanton (1918-1942) only had a couple of years of active influence on jazz history. Both died from tuberculosis. During Blanton's time with Duke Ellington, from 1939 until 1941, he recorded with the band, and with Duke in piano and bass duets. *Jack the Bear* was his feature with the full band. 'Bear' was saxophonist Ben Webster's name for Blanton.

The best known duo track is *Pitter Panther Patter*. Like Christian, Blanton took part in the informal jam sessions at Minton's Playhouse in New York. His playing inspired subsequent important bass players, particularly Ray Brown, Charles Mingus and Oscar Pettiford. Blanton had a strong tone with a powerful sense of swing. He led the way for bassists to escape from the 'walking bass' solo style then prevalent.

Django Reinhardt

One of the few non-American musicians to have a major effect on the history of jazz before World War II was Django Reinhardt (1910-1953). He was French, though born in Belgium. The son of a traveling entertainer, he grew up in a gypsy settlement outside Paris.

Django is said to have heard no jazz until he encountered Louis Armstrong's *Dallas Blues* when he was twenty years old. In 1928 Django lost the use of two fingers of his left hand as a result of a caravan fire, but overcame this by developing an idiosyncratic compensatory technique. With violinist Stephane Grappelli (1908-1997) he formed the Quintette du Hot Club de France in 1934, an ensemble of violin, three guitars and double bass. In 1935, Django recorded with Coleman Hawkins (*Stardust*), changed to electric guitar during the 1940s, and toured America with Duke Ellington in 1946.

Coleman Hawkins

Coleman Hawkins (1901-1969) was taught piano from the age of five. Later he learned cello, and began on tenor saxophone at nine. His first job was playing in the orchestra of the 12th Street Theater in Kansas City in 1921.

In 1924 and 1925 Louis Armstrong was a featured soloist with the Fletcher Henderson band, at the time when Coleman Hawkins was also a soloist with Henderson. Hawkins's tenor saxophone style subsequently owed more to Armstrong's trumpet than to any other saxophonists. In fact there were few saxophonists on which Hawkins could model himself, meaning that he pioneered a defining style for the tenor saxophone. Saxophonist Russ Gershon has expressed the idea that Hawkins's style came from classical music. "He started out on cello and I think his saxophone innovations were his transferring romantic cello music onto the tenor saxophone." [9]

Hawkins spent ten years with Fletcher Henderson, before moving to England in 1934, initially appearing there with Jack Hylton's band. Hawkins worked also in Paris and Zürich. His great prewar performance, both a commercial and artistic success, was of two improvised choruses on *Body and Soul* recorded in 1939 upon his return to America. At the end of 1939, readers of *Down Beat* magazine voted Hawkins 'Best Tenor Saxophonist.'

Fats Waller

Alligator Crawl, Handful of Keys, Numb Fumblin', Smashing Thirds, Valentine Stomp and *Viper's Drag* are all compositions of

Thomas 'Fats' Waller (1904-1943), in the stride tradition. Add his successful popular songs, which include *Ain't Misbehavin', Honeysuckle Rose, Jitterbug Waltz* and *Your Feet's Too Big* and there is ample evidence to support the assertion that Waller's greatest importance lies in his compositions. Yet he was a wonderful improviser, jazz singer and an entertainer with great charm.

"I had never seen anybody like Fats, who was well over six feet tall and weighed over three hundred pounds...and was larger than life anyway, and was a tremendously vital presence...it was impossible not to be carried away by his very engaging personality, and by just the rhythmic force of what he was doing. He made that piano jump, he was in constant motion." [10] It is a surprise to be reminded that Fats died while still in his thirties.

Count Basie

A musician who studied informally with Fats Waller, pianist and bandleader William 'Count' Basie (1904-1984) came from Red Bank, New Jersey, though the style of his famous and influential band had its origins in Kansas City. Basie was stranded in the city while touring in 1927. In 1929 he joined Bennie Moten's Kansas City Orchestra. After Moten's death in 1935, Basie organized a new, smaller group of nine musicians, which included bassist Walter Page, drummer Jo Jones and later, tenor saxophonist Lester Young. Soon the Count Basie Orchestra, as it became known, was one of the leading bands. Important recordings included *One O'Clock Jump* (1937), *Jumpin' at the Woodside* (1938 - named after the Woodside hotel), and *Taxi War Dance* (1939).

Lester Young

Much of the interest and excitement of these Basie sides stems from the contribution of Lester Young (1909-1959). "Lester was the prototypical hipster," observed Dan Morgenstern. "He walked on crepe soles, gliding through life like a graceful sleepwalker. Porkpie hats became fashionable long after he had introduced them. His detached yet knowing attitude became a model for a generation of 'cool' people. Lester created a revolution in jazz long before any official revolt was announced. It was a quiet revolution, a profound change in sensibility, a new way of employing rhythmic and melodic freedom, a different approach to the production of sound. Lester soared over the crescendo of the Basie band in full cry with beautiful, logical, astonishing, and perfectly placed phrases. His playing was the essence of streamlining - a design concept which, perhaps not coincidentally, made its public appearance at the time of Lester's record debut." [11]

Young emerged alongside Buck Clayton, Jimmy Rushing, Herschel Evans and Oran Hot Lips Page, in the Count Basie Band. Lester claimed that his influence was Frankie Trumbauer's C-Melody saxophone playing. Nicknamed Prez, short for President of the saxophone players, Lester spelled it with a 'z', as one can see from his own signature on the provenance card accompanying his Conn saxophone in the collection at the Institute of Jazz Studies, Rutgers University.

Appropriately for a 'graceful sleepwalker', Young's style was cooler than most, with a less rich tone, more spare vibrato, and a choice of notes that was linear, rather than vertical. Prez's importance was that he offered an alternative to the rich and intense style of Coleman Hawkins. Lester left Basie in 1940. Though still a young man, his best and most influential work was probably already on record. The list of saxophone players he influenced is enormous, including Al Cohn, Stan Getz, Dexter Gordon, Jimmy Guiffre, Charlie Parker, Zoot Sims and Sonny Stitt.

Lester Young held his saxophone out away from his body, similar to the way that a flute player holds the instrument. This horizontal hold was because Prez liked to play the saxophone in bed; he held it that way to keep it clear of the bedclothes.

The British trumpet player Dick Hawdon (b. 1927) gives a European perspective on Lester's physical decline. They shared a concert in 1953: "Norman Granz brought them all to the Kilburn State (London) for the Canvey Island Flood Relief concerts. That was Jazz at the Philharmonic, with Lester Young, Stan Getz, Flip Phillips, Charlie Shavers and the Oscar Peterson Trio. The real surprise was that Lester came on without a hat. He shuffled on. He had gout in both legs." [12] Lester was only 44.

Bunny Berigan

Rowland Bernart 'Bunny' Berigan (1908-1942) trumpeter and bandleader was influenced both by Bix Beiderbecke and Louis Armstrong. His obituary printed in the *New York Times* for Wednesday, June 3, 1942 tells most of his story:

"Bernard (Bunny) Berigan, 33-year-old orchestra leader and trumpet player, died early yesterday morning in the Polyclinic Hospital, where he was taken on Monday. He was stricken Sunday night with an intestinal ailment at the Van Cortlandt Hotel, 142 West Forty-ninth Street, where he made his home.

The orchestra leader who became well known by distinctive trumpet-playing during the jitterbug era, first became ill on April 20th while on tour in Pennsylvania. After spending two weeks in a Pittsburgh hospital he was warned against playing his trumpet. His final collapse was attributed to his insistence on playing the instrument that won him his success as a soloist in a number of famous name bands before organizing his own band. Mr. Berigan was born at Fox Lake, Wis., and earned his living playing the violin and trumpet from the time he was 14. Since his graduation from the University of Wisconsin he had appeared as a feature soloist with Rudy Vallee, Tommy Dorsey, Abe Lyman, Benny Goodman and Paul Whiteman. His best known recording, which became his theme song, is I Can't Get Started With You. *Since organizing his own orchestra five years ago, Mr. Berigan played his trumpet in nearly every number, and directed the orchestra at the same time."* [13]

What this extract from Berigan's obituary does not tell is that the 'intestinal ailment' was alcohol-related but, more importantly, that he was an inspiring trumpet soloist with an uninhibited style, a wide range and beautiful tone. His most acclaimed recordings are *I Can't Get Started*, under his own name, and a 1937 recording of *Marie*, with the Tommy Dorsey Orchestra.

Blue Note Records

The Blue Note record label was started by Alfred Lion and Frances Wolff in 1939. The immediate aim was to record Art Hodes and George Lewis, their favorites. They began by issuing a disc by soprano saxophonist Sidney Bechet, of Gershwin's *Summertime*, and eventually succeeded in documenting a major slice of jazz history. True to their original aim, they recorded much traditional jazz and swing, with James P. Johnson, Edmond Hall, Ike Quebec and Tiny Grimes.

The company was one of the earliest to use 12" 78 rpm discs to cope with longer performances. The label then went on to be one of the first record companies to capture the music of bop musicians, including Thelonious Monk. The coming of the LP was embraced by Blue Note, and albums were issued by Grant Green, Freddie Hubbard, Jackie McLean, Horace Silver, Jimmy Smith and Stanley Turrentine. Into the 1960s, artists in their catalog included Herbie Hancock, Andrew Hill, Wayne Shorter and McCoy Tyner. Blue Note was indirectly acquired by EMI in 1980, and a new generation of jazz musicians was added to the Blue Note roster. Among them were Bobby McFerrin, Michel Petrucciani, and Stanley Jordan (b. 1959), a guitarist who used a two-handed tapping technique known as 'the touch', first introduced by Jimmy Webster in the 1950s.

Billie Holiday

The early life of Billie Holiday (1915-1959) is something of a mystery. For whatever reasons, her autobiography is inaccurate, and her father, guitarist Clarence Holiday, refused to acknowledge her until she achieved success. "Don't talk about Billie in front of all the guys," he is reported as saying. "They'll think I'm old. She was something I stole when I was fourteen." [14]

She began singing in New York clubs in 1930, and in 1933 was discovered by the famous and wealthy jazz enthusiast and record producer John Hammond, who was part of the Vanderbilt family. Other artists whose careers Hammond launched were Charlie Christian, George Benson, Aretha Franklin, Bob Dylan and Bruce Springsteen. Hammond immediately organized three recording sessions for Billie Holiday, with Benny Goodman. That year she appeared as an extra in a Paul Robeson film, *The Emperor Jones.* She also played some parts in a radio soap opera, and made a short film with the Duke Ellington band, *Symphony in Black.* In 1934 and 1935 she had successful engagements at the Apollo Theater in Harlem.

She recorded with Teddy Wilson and Lester Young, joined Count Basie in 1937, then Artie Shaw in 1938. Billie's recordings made in the 1930s and 1940s contain some magnificent work, performances which have endured and appealed across generations in a way that no other jazz singer - indeed, no other singer of any genre - can equal. Though she has a small voice and a modest range she communicates intimately and emotionally, effectively using space and a behind-the-beat delivery. Hear *Any Old Time*, with the Artie Shaw band, *Strange Fruit* and *Fine and Mellow* (1939), and *Lover Man* (1944).

Ella Fitzgerald

If Louis Armstrong invented scat singing - the singing of a quasi-instrumental improvised line using nonsense syllables - it was Ella Fitzgerald (1918-1996) who set generations of singers wanting to master that art. Ella was sensational at scatting, able to improvise chorus after chorus, ever swinging, ever in tune.

A model for all jazz singers, Ella was discovered in 1934 in an amateur show at the Apollo Theater in Harlem. This led directly to work with the band of drummer Chick Webb. When Webb died in 1939, Ella took over the leadership of the band for the next three years. In 1946 she began appearing as part of impresario Norman Granz's touring package *Jazz at the Philharmonic*. This introduced her to international audiences. She developed a worldwide following.

In several senses Ella was the antithesis of Billie Holiday. Ella possessed an innate cheerfulness, which restricted her range of emotional expression. Billie had intensity and pathos. Ella's voice was somewhat girlish in timbre. Billie's voice was that of a worldly woman. Ella scatted with the technical competence that matched some of the best jazz instrumentalists. Billie's jazziness resided in her simple paraphrasing of a melody. Yet both possessed that one quality shared by all world-class jazz musicians: each needs to perform only half a bar of music to be recognized.

Harlem Today

Until recently, Harlem was a depressed economic area with considerable unemployment, much of its housing substandard. Yet with the return of middle-class blacks to the neighborhood there has been some gentrification. Now the area faces a more prosperous future. Harlem is in the midst of what some have called the Second Harlem Renaissance, a renewal of culture, commerce and tourism. Significantly, in August 2001, former President Bill Clinton opened his post-White House office at 55 West 125th Street.

Furthermore, in 2002, the intention to develop a National Jazz Museum in Harlem was announced. Saxophonist and jazz historian Loren Schoenberg was named as the Museum's first director. Congress voted $1 million start-up money for the project. The museum's mission is to preserve Harlem's invaluable jazz heritage for future generations. Harlem has played an important role in the development of American jazz. It is the ideal location for the jazz museum.

References
1.   Spencer, F. J., *Jazz and Death* (Mississippi: University of Mississippi Press, 2002), p. 64.
2.   Walser, R., *Keeping Time; Readings in Jazz History* (Oxford University Press, 1999), p. 10.
3.   Ibid., p. 11.
4.   Shapiro, N. and Hentoff, N., op. cit., p. 181.
5.   Schuller, G., *Early Jazz,* op. cit., p. 192, note 21.
6.   Ibid.

7. Lees, G., *Arranging the Score* (London: Cassell, 2000), p. 146.
8. Morgenstern, D., from *Art Tatum: God Is In the House*. Liner notes, Onyx records, 1973.
9. Stokes, W. Royal, *Living the Jazz Life* (Oxford University Press, 2002), p. 56.
10. Dan Morgenstern interview, with Janet Sommer, 'All About Jazz' website.
11. Morgenstern, D., op. cit., from *Jazz People,* 1976.
12. Brown, J. R. 'No Motorways at All'. Interview with Dick Hawdon, *Jazz Review,* July 2002, p. 17.
13. *New York Times,* Wednesday, June 3, 1942.
14. Clarke, D., 'Billie Holiday', *Down Beat*, vol. 69, No. 8, August, 2002, p. 23.

5. *Concert at Carnegie*

Tonight is Sunday evening, 16 January, 1938. We are standing at Fifty Seventh and Seventh in Midtown Manhattan, outside Carnegie Hall. Strictly a classical music venue, Tchaikovsky himself conducted at its inaugural concert in 1891. On the large billboards outside are details of several concerts, an announcement of a violin recital, together with information about the 1937-38 season of Young People's Concerts, with performances of the Scherzo from Mendelssohn's *Midsummer Night's Dream* and the Rondo from Mozart's *Bassoon Concerto*. One poster is different, proclaiming: 'The First Swing Concert in the History of Carnegie Hall.'

Yes, jazz now enters these august surroundings. We are fortunate to be among the 3,900 that have tickets, for the concert has been sold out for days. This is because Benny Goodman and his Swing Orchestra are appearing. Today, swing's the thing. The twenty- eight year old Goodman and his colleagues are big with the nation's youth. Some say that Benny Goodman's name is better known than that of President Roosevelt. Benny, 'King of Swing', is rumored to be a millionaire already. His income was reported last year to be around a hundred thousand dollars.

We have all been buying the clarinetist's brilliant records after listening to his radio broadcasts. Some people here were in the audience last March (1937) when the band played for two weeks at the Paramount Theater. That was popular. When the musicians arrived at the theater on the first morning, for a 7:00 a.m. rehearsal, people were already waiting in line for tickets. The band played five shows a day, for two weeks.

Now, the prospect of actually seeing these famous young musicians in concert is creating an electric atmosphere. Tonight there is a bonus. Other musicians are here at Carnegie Hall, including cohorts from the Count Basie Band and the Duke Ellington Orchestra.

Look along the line waiting outside the hall. The audience, though youthful, will appear strangely mature to later generations. The weather is cold; all these young men and women wear expensive hats, and good, long, overcoats. When we get inside, the hall is so full that an overflow section of one hundred seats (at $2.20 a chair) is arranged on the stage. Many of the women in that section wear hats. Some even wear veils, which are fashionable. Journalists dub these folk sophisti-cats!

The concert was tremendous, but *Down Beat* magazine (15 cents a copy) had a headline that said 'Benny's Clarinet Sounds Good to Lorgnettes - Band a Bit Shaky.' Shaky or not, many said that it is a pity that there was no recording made of the concert.

Later - years later - we discovered that there was. One of the first jazz LPs, it appeared in mono twelve years after the concert! The recording is sensational; it was *Down Beat's* reporting that had been a bit shaky. The band sounded magnificent.

The Swing Era

Swing is another word for jazz. Artie Shaw had nitpicked at the use of the word, saying that, "Jazz must swing, and if it doesn't swing it isn't jazz. That's why swing is, as far as I'm concerned, a verb, not an adjective and not a noun." [1]

The swing era was the time of the greatest popularity of jazz, when jazz *was* the pop music of the day. It was the time of the big band, but not all big bands played undiluted jazz. In ten years, the skills of the arrangers had developed to the stage where the best bands played a sophisticated music that combined virtuosity, complexity and a true jazz feel. The greatest bands were those of Cab Calloway, Count Basie, the Dorsey Brothers, Duke Ellington, Erskine Hawkins, Jimmie Lunceford, Artie Shaw, Claude Thornhill and, of course, Benny Goodman.

The stereotype was a big band able to play for both dancing and listening, led by a virtuoso instrumentalist, featuring jazz soloists among its personnel, plus a singer or two. Famous singers from this period included Ella Fitzgerald, Billie Holiday, Peggy Lee and Mel Tormé. Frank Sinatra began his career as a band singer, with the virtuoso trumpet and trombone player Tommy Dorsey, from whom Sinatra learned the skill of diaphragm breathing - not, as a BBC radio jazz presenter once claimed - circular breathing!

The Great Depression hung over America from 1929 until 1934. 'By the summer of 1935, America was beginning to experience a feeling of hope and a sense of relief from the misery of the previous six years, which had an unemployment rate of 25 percent, a failed stock market, soup kitchens, and people riding the rails and hitchhiking along the nation's highways in search of a fresh start.' [2] Thus the bands had to strive hard to entertain. This is the explanation for the slick presentation, the band uniforms, the communicative announcements, the onstage hokum, the multiple vocalists and singing groups drawn from within the band, the medleys, and the virtuoso band leader.

The best popular songs of the day lent themselves well to jazz improvisation. The great popular songwriters Harold Arlen, Irving Berlin, Hoagy Carmichael, George Gershwin, Jerome Kern, Cole Porter and Richard Rodgers composed the chord progressions on which the melodies were built in a way that suited jazz improvisation perfectly. The best tunes had a sophistication that appealed to inquisitive musicians. *Body and Soul*, written in 1930 by Johnny Green, was typical. Recorded by Coleman Hawkins, Benny Goodman and many others, it has a rich chord progression. The key scheme in the release is both ingenious and pleasing.

The swing era began in the mid-thirties, at the conclusion of the Depression. It ended during World War II. Swing music was important in dispelling the darkness and hopelessness of the post-Depression period, and in maintaining morale during the terrors and uncertainties of the early war years.

Those who are critical of the music of this period forget the context in which it flourished. Jazz, a freewheeling music that encouraged the unfettered expression of the individual, also symbolized the struggle that the war represented, so much so that the Nazis banned the word 'jazz' in occupied Europe. Goebbels even ordered the Nazi propaganda ministry to organize its own swing band to broadcast familiar tunes with new anti-Semitic lyrics in English. Dave Brubeck later observed that jazz expresses the United States, and represents freedom. "It's more important than baseball," he said. [3]

In part, the conflict was about the racism of the Nazis, who reached new depths in their persecution of Jews, gypsies, homosexuals and Negroes. American Negroes saw a great paradox, for the American fighting forces still suffered racial segregation within their military organization. Some jobs in the defense industry remained closed to blacks. After the war the returning troops were aghast to suffer racism on their own soil. The continuation of white supremacy was not an appropriate outcome for those who had been fighting racism abroad.

Now, intolerance and bigotry were rooted out and gradually removed, though not without some notorious incidents. Black musicians became more assertive. Some said that the common use of the term 'man', used by the boppers, came about as a counter to the term 'boy' which had long been used by whites addressing blacks. This older form of address is preserved in songs of the era. *Chattanooga Choo Choo* begins, "Pardon Me, Boy."

This was still an issue in 1959, when the British trumpet player Dick Hawdon appeared at the Newport Jazz Festival with Johnny Dankworth and his Orchestra, and a week of double concerts with the Ellington band. "I was talking to Johnny Hodges at the side, by the wire," said Dick. "Two blue-rinsed ladies came up. One said to him: 'Could you be a good boy and get me Duke's autograph?' 'Madam, how can I be a boy? I'm 52,' he said, and walked away. I wondered what had offended him. It took me five minutes to realize that it was the 'boy' bit." [4]

At the head of the swing movement was a brilliant young clarinetist from Chicago, Benny Goodman (1909-1986), the King of Swing. August 21, 1935, was the date that Benny Goodman's band reached Los Angeles to play an engagement at the Palomar Ballroom. The musicians arrived to see an enormous throng of people lined up around the block. The band had been heard coast to coast on a radio program, *Let's Dance*, sponsored by the Nabisco company. Their reputation had preceded them. Within weeks of the Palomar engagement three of Benny Goodman's records were in the Top Ten in the California record shops.

Jazz has many players with titles - including *Earl* Hines, *King* Oliver, *Lady* Day, *Count* Basie, *Duke* Ellington, *Sir* Charles Thompson and *Sir* Roland Hanna. Paul Whiteman was called *King* of Jazz, Bessie Smith *Empress* of the Blues, Artie Shaw *King* of the Clarinet, and Benny

Goodman named *King of Swing*. No one can dispute Goodman's ability as a clarinet player. He is undoubtedly one of the great virtuosi of the twentieth century. For proof of this, hear Goodman's recordings of the classical works he commissioned: Copland's *Concerto*, Bartók's *Contrasts*, Morton Feldman's *Derivations* and several other technically challenging pieces which testify to his outstanding command of the instrument. He was a professional jazz musician while still in his early teens. His first recording was made before his eighteenth birthday. Even then, he had an enviable ability to swing, combined with a sure idea of what sounded good on the clarinet.

Benny was one of a family of nine children, his father a poor hard working émigré from Poland. Eventually, Benny married the sister of John Hammond, thus entering one of the aristocratic families of America. But he was a sensational clarinet player from the beginning. "The first time I heard Benny Goodman was in Chicago when he was a kid of eight or nine, and he was doing an imitation of Ted Lewis, who, of course, was then the king," said Ben Pollack. "Later, at fifteen or sixteen, and just before I brought him to the Coast to work with me at the Venice Ballroom, he was playing a mixture of Jimmy Noone, Leon Rappolo, Buster Bailey, and other great clarinet players. He always had a terrific gift for handling his instrument, that combination of technique and tone, plus the one thing every musician seeks - a style that can be identified before his name is announced. That style is his own, and he developed it himself." [5]

The public awareness of swing, the enthusiasm for the big band combined with the discovery that this was wonderful music for dancing, all seemed to lock into place with Goodman. Jazz is an art form, not an athletic activity. There can never be a greatest, or best, practitioner.

Anyone who thinks that to be louder, higher or faster is to be better is neglecting the most important dimension, *depth*. To follow that line of thinking is to behave as thoughtlessly as classical radio stations who trivialize the great music they claim to celebrate by broadcasting top ten lists!

Once that is understood, any terms such as greatest or best - or, yes, *King of Swing* - become meaningless. Some believe that Artie Shaw was more modern, and had a greater melodic gift, than Benny. They point to Shaw's massive hit records, *Frenesi* and *Begin the Beguine*. Goodman did not have such national hits. Others argue that Count Basie's band, with Lester Young, bassist Walter Page, drummer Jo Jones and guitarist Freddie Green, was the band that really swung, that it was Basie who merited the title *King of Swing*. For a while even Louis Armstrong took exception to Benny Goodman being called *King of Swing*. He felt - with justification - that he was King.

Although Louis Armstrong was the first to record with a racially mixed band, when he made *Knockin' A Jug* (with Jack Teagarden) in 1929, Benny Goodman was not far behind. He recorded with a racially mixed band in 1933. Goodman was the first to perform a jazz concert in Carnegie Hall. More important, it was Benny Goodman who had the enormous popular success, who was the recipient of the Beatlemania of his day. And so Benny Goodman was dubbed *King of Swing* by the fans and writers. In the final analysis, the debate is pointless. History cannot be changed, however worthy or justified the claims of others, however silly the title under dispute. Benny Goodman was called *King of Swing* in his day. That is what we call him now.

Showbiz memories are short. In the mid-1970s the American baseball star Babe Ruth was the subject of a book called 'The King of Swing.' The book had nothing to do with music.

Why Was Benny Goodman Important?

• Goodman's 1938 concert in Carnegie Hall was a break-through, opening up the possibility of Carnegie Hall concerts to Duke Ellington, Woody Herman, and other jazz musicians. However, it must be remembered that an all-Negro band under the leadership of James Reese Europe had appeared at Carnegie two decades earlier.

• Benny Goodman energized racial integration in jazz, both by hiring pianist Teddy Wilson and vibraphonist Lionel Hampton to play to a paying audience in the mid-thirties, but also by hiring black arrangers Fletcher Henderson, Jimmy Mundy and Edgar Sampson.

• The concept of a small group within a big band (trio, quartet and sextet) was introduced by Goodman.

• Goodman was one of the great instrumentalists of the twentieth century.

Boogie-Woogie

Boogie-woogie is a solo piano style that grew out of ragtime and stride. Usually (but not inevitably) associated with a twelve bar blues progression, the essence of boogie-woogie is the left hand ostinato bass of pairs of repeated eighth notes. Ostinato means obstinate or persistent. It refers to an unyielding rhythmic or melodic figure - in this case, the propulsive left hand. Many printed antecedents of boogie-woogie are extant from the early 1900s. Clarence 'Pinetop' Smith (1904-1929) recorded *Pinetop's Boogie-Woogie* in 1928. He was shot dead accidentally at 25. Sadly, no photograph exists of this wonderful pianist.

A boogie-woogie craze flourished in the 1930s, when John Hammond brought Albert Ammons and Meade 'Lux' Lewis away from their jobs as Chicago taxi drivers. With Pete Johnson, they were the popular boogie-woogie pianists of the day. Meade 'Lux' Lewis recorded *Honky Tonk Train Blues* in 1937. Jimmy Yancey (1894-1951) recorded a series of piano solos in 1939. Many of the big bands - Count Basie, Benny Goodman, Tommy Dorsey, Harry James - included boogie-woogie items in their repertoires during the swing era. The interest in boogie-woogie lasted long enough for British revivalist trumpeter Humphrey Lyttelton to get his *Bad Penny Blues* into the Top Twenty of the UK Charts in 1956.

Artie Shaw

Artie Shaw (b. 1910) was Benny Goodman's great rival. He, too, was a brilliant clarinet-playing bandleader who enjoyed great popular acclaim. His big hits included *Frenesi* and *Begin the Beguine*. Shaw is a man of considerable accomplishment, a restless individual. In all, Artie has been married eight times. He had four celebrity wives, Lana Turner, Ava Gardner, Evelyn Keyes and Kathleen Winsor, author of *Forever Amber*. He and Judy Garland were an item for a while.

Not only did Shaw refine his clarinet playing to a dazzling technical standard, particularly in the top register, but he managed to develop a tone quality on the clarinet that was unmistakably his own. Shaw knew how to give an exciting performance. He was an accomplished arranger and songwriter (he wrote the words and music for *Any Old Time* for Billie Holiday to sing when she was in his band), but is also a published author. He has written a collection of three short novels about love gone bad, *I Love, I Hate You, Drop Dead*. Of more relevance to jazz history is his 1952 book *The Trouble with Cinderella; An Outline of Identity,* an all too true account of the twin pulls of art and commerce on a musician in popular music, still pertinent now. In 1955 Shaw gave up playing to go to live on the Mediterranean coast at Bagur in Spain, in a house he had designed himself. He fished avidly, studied the guitar, and became good at small-bore rifle shooting. He studied astronomy.

In 1960 he returned to America. Though he took an interest in an Artie Shaw band led by reed player Dick Johnson, and appeared at various conferences and seminars as a speaker, he never played again. In 2002 Shaw spoke at the International Association for Jazz Education 29th Annual Conference in Long Beach, California. Just a few weeks short of his ninety-second birthday, Shaw was articulate, outspoken, opinionated, combative and entertainingly funny. For those of us attending that seminar it was easy to understand how forceful Shaw must have been in his youth.

At one point in his career Artie Shaw ran a big band with strings. He was not the only swing era bandleader to present an extra large ensemble. This raises the question of whether there is a standard size for a big band. By 1944, Glenn Miller (1904-1944) had a big band with eight brass and five saxes. He also ran a concert orchestra, which was a full big band with an added string section and horns. In the late 1940s, Stan Kenton's band was the last word in modernity. Kenton (1911-1979) added a section of mellophoniums to the conventional big band instrumentation. A mellophonium is a sort of mellophone, with the bell facing forward.

Listeners are divided on Kenton's music. Some are still of the opinion that it represents a major plateau of achievement in the history of the jazz orchestra. Others have expressed the view that Kenton's efforts were the musical equivalent of fascist architecture! George Frazier's opinion was that "The Kenton orchestra was neither fish nor flesh, but pretty foul." [6] Hear it, and come to your own conclusions.

At the beginning of the twenty-first century a big band or jazz orchestra is typically eight brass (four trumpets, four trombones), five saxophones (two altos, two tenors and a baritone) and four rhythm instruments - normally piano, bass, guitar and drums. There are variations on this instrumentation. Woody Herman used one alto, three tenors and baritone for his saxophone section. Arranger Thad Jones chose the soprano saxophone, rather than the alto, to lead his saxes.

Californian arranger Bob Florence calls for six saxophones, adding a second baritone. The Canadian arranger Rob McConnell includes flugelhorns, flutes and vibraphone in his scores. Despite these exceptions, when a big band is discussed most people have the standard seventeen piece ensemble in mind.

The enormous popularity of the big bands meant full employment for musicians. For some, the swing era was the finest moment of jazz. The classic well-crafted songs of the great songwriters were performed by virtuoso instrumentalists in polished ensembles. Big bands were big news. Enthusiasm for big bands lingered on for decades among circles of dedicated fans. Even into the present century there are swing bands on the road all over the world, 'ghost' ensembles recreating the sound of the swing bands, Glenn Miller's in particular. This longevity was reinforced by nostalgia connected with the war, the great emotional intensity of the times, the camaraderie and kinship, the high quality of the best of the songs of that era, and the power of popular music as symbolic of the age.

For those with ears to listen, plus an open mind, there is no disputing the greatness of the best of the big bands. Yet some commentators have been unfairly harsh. This is frequently the case when an aspect of jazz attracts public acclaim. A jazz performer only has to achieve commercial success to be the target of critical snipes: consider Benny Goodman, Dave Brubeck, or the Bossa Nova success of Stan Getz.

Glenn Miller in particular has received a bad press, fueled by thoughtless comments from some who should have known better. Only recently, in Gunther Schuller's excellent and enthusiastic reappraisal of Glenn Miller's work, has Miller's contribution to the development of the big band been intelligently evaluated. [7]

For a musician, to be caught in the commercial atmosphere of the swing era was not necessarily good news. The age-old conflict between art and commerce raged; rarely can the needs of both be satisfied. The big bands provided much lucrative work, but offered little or no platform for experimental soloists, or composers or arrangers who attempted to fashion their own personal styles. That had to be done after hours, away from broadcasts, movies and concert halls.

The Japanese attack on the American fleet in Pearl Harbor, Hawaii, on 7 December, 1941, outraged America. The USA joined the conflict against the Axis powers. The entertainment industry, to which jazz belonged at that time, was changed permanently, along with everything else in the world. A symbolic moment occurred during a concert played by the Artie Shaw band at the Metropole Theater in Providence, Rhode Island, a naval base on the east coast of the USA, north of New York. Shaw was asked by the theater manager to announce to all service personnel in the audience that they had to report to their bases immediately. The result was a mass exodus from the theater. An incredulous Shaw canceled the rest of the concert. Shaw went on to front a naval band which toured the Pacific in 1943-44, until he was medically discharged. Shaw later stated that, "My career as a serious dedicated player of a musical instrument ended in 1941." [8]

After the war, the whole world of entertainment changed totally. "The steadily decreasing demand for big bands began in the early summer of 1946," observed Harry James's biographer Peter Levinson. "Attendance at ballrooms, night clubs and one nighters declined sharply.

Wartime prosperity had ended. Veterans, as well as young people, were saving their money to buy houses and appliances instead of spending it going out to dance. It was the rise of the singers and their seizure of the public's interest that was of paramount importance." [9]

Though their popularity had waned, bands such as those of Count Basie (notably with the *Atomic Mr Basie* album of 1957, composed and arranged by the underrated Neal Hefti), Lionel Hampton (1908-2002), Woody Herman (1913-1987), Harry James, Stan Kenton and Duke Ellington continued to tour the world, giving concerts into the 1960s. Duke Ellington played the Newport Jazz Festival to great success in 1956 and 1957. The British Ted Heath band toured America and played Carnegie Hall. The Les Brown band had a permanent spot on the Bob Hope Show on radio. The Benny Goodman big band visited the USSR in 1962. But the swing era was gone, the big swing bands no longer popular. After ten years of postwar struggle the final blow was the arrival of rock 'n' roll and the rise in popularity of the electric guitar, in the mid-1950s.

This was not the end of the large ensemble as an artistic force in jazz. A continuous line of great jazz composers and arrangers maintained the evolution and development of the jazz orchestra to the end of the twentieth century. Though mostly rehearsal bands that played for fun or for limited spells of professional work, they made occasional appearances at festivals and conferences. These included the bands of Toshiko Akiyoshi, Django Bates, Bob Berg, Francy Boland, Bob Brookmeyer, John Dankworth, Don Ellis, Gil Evans, Bob Florence, Mike Gibbs, Peter Herbolzheimer, Bill Holman, Thad Jones, Rob McConnell, Oliver Nelson, Lennie Niehaus, Marty Paich, Bill Russo, Maria Schneider, Martial Solal, Stan Tracey, Kenny Wheeler and Gerald Wilson.

Large ensembles have also proved popular in the many colleges and universities that offer jazz education courses. A student jazz orchestra presents an opportunity for a low cost activity, as one tutor can direct up to twenty students for two or three hours at a time. The jazz orchestra provides a mixed ability ensemble that sounds good, and for which there is an enormous repertoire of published material available, covering the complete history of the music, if not the complete range of styles. Additionally, other study areas can be linked to a jazz orchestra. These include composition, orchestration, arranging and musical direction. As an ensemble it is ideal for accompanying visiting jazz performers.

References

1. Soar, R., 'The Beguine Begins Again', *Jazz Journal International*, December, 1984.
2. Levinson, P., *Trumpet Blues, The Life of Harry James* (OUP, 1999).
3. Burns, K., *Jazz*. TV documentary.
4. Brown, J. R., op. cit., p.17.
5. Shapiro, N. and Hentoff, N., op. cit., p. 126.
6. Easton, C., *Straight Ahead: The Story of Stan Kenton* (New York: William Morrow, 1973).
7. Schuller, G., *The Swing Era* (OUP, 1989), pp. 661- 677.
8. Shaw, A., quoted in Lees, G., *Meet Me at Jim and Andy's: Jazz Musicians and Their World* (OUP, 1988), pp. 84 -5.
9. Levinson, P., op. cit., p. 162.

6. Bebop, Bird, and the Birth of the Cool

We are in Midtown Manhattan, between Fifth and Sixth Avenues, on 52nd Street. The year is 1945, the year of the death (in April) of President Roosevelt, in his fourth term, having served twelve years. Musicians have gathered here in the 52nd Street area since Bix Beiderbecke's time. These few hundred yards of highway are currently the jazz capital of the world, with seven cellar clubs in one block - the Downbeat, the Famous Door, the Onyx, Jimmy Ryan's, the Spotlite, the Three Deuces and the Troc. Known as 'The Street', there have been clubs here since the early thirties. They will continue until the late forties - legendary names such as the Hickory House and Kelly's Stable.

World War II is almost at an end, which explains the presence of many people in military uniform, both in the audience and among some of the musicians hanging out. In Dan Morgenstern's words: "When intramural competition among club-owners had reached its peak, it was possible to take a stroll from the corner of Sixth Avenue up to '21', and backtrack on the other side to the White Rose Bar, accompanied by the strains of Billie Holiday, Art Tatum, Charlie Parker, Coleman Hawkins, Lester Young, Hot Lips Page - and then some. Sitting in was taken for granted. During the height of the holy bop wars, George Brunies marched himself out of Ryan's and blasted off on his trombone in the direction of Dizzy's habitat across the street, challenging him to a musical duel, traffic be damned. Diz declined." [1]

Here in the clubs we see many of the people we read about in *Down Beat* and *Metronome*. By moving from club to club, in the space of an hour or so we hear several of the giants of jazz. Some of the musicians we hear seem to be interested in modernity, where jazz is heading next, for this is a testing ground for the new, a place where each player's ideas and techniques are put to work against the competition. However, everybody plays here. There are New Orleans and swing styles to be heard as well as the experiments of Parker and Gillespie. At times The Street is wild, with its inflammatory mix of alcohol and race.

At home we listen to jazz on 78 records, but not everyone has a phonograph. Record collections can be small. For a while, recently, it has been difficult to keep up with what is happening in modern jazz, because no new jazz recordings have been issued. From August 1942 there was an American Federation of Musicians ban on all recording by instrumentalists. This lasted for more than two years.

Today, in the early 2000s, the clubs are long gone, and that section of 52nd Street is lined with luxurious office buildings. When I walked the area with Dan Morgenstern, during the writing of this book, the only hint of The Street's history was beneath our feet. Overhead, there is much to gaze at, but if you resist looking upwards as you walk through midtown on The Street you will see several polished black granite tablets let into the sidewalk. Each one bears the name of one of the musicians who played here at the start of the modern jazz movement - Art Tatum, Miles Davis, Dizzy Gillespie, Bud Powell, Thelonious Monk, Charlie Parker, Lester Young, Billie Holiday and Sarah Vaughan. In 1979 it was renamed Swing Street.

Musically, many of the melodies and improvisations of the new modernists were based on strings of eighth notes, and frequently ended on a pair of eighth notes, the second of the two accented. As the musicians were regularly singing these phrases to each other, they did

93

what musicians always do: they sang appropriate rhythmic nonsense syllables, not *la la la!* Many of these eighth note melodic scraps ended with the word 'rebop', or something that sounded very close. The new music was quickly christened 'rebop', or 'bebop', soon reduced to 'bop'.

The unfamiliar modern jazz certainly sounded different. Some said that bebop offered greater virtuosity. To an extent that was true, but instrumental limitations have been challenged throughout jazz history. From Louis Armstrong's projection of the trumpet range above high C, to Jimmy Blanton's redefinition of the capabilities of the double bass - not to mention the astonishing pianism of Art Tatum - jazz players had continually advanced instrumental techniques.

Some commentators have claimed that this was the first time that jazz musicians had based their solos on the chords of a tune, rather than the melody. Again, that was not true; just listen. From Louis Armstrong to Benny Goodman to Bud Freeman, soloists had been improvising on the harmonies rather than the tune. The difference was that the modern jazz combined several elements in an unusual way. Certainly, tempos were more extreme. Performances were longer. Small groups predominated. Clarinet and rhythm guitar were no longer fashionable. Arranged music was less predominant; front line instruments usually played the theme in unison. Bebop was more aggressive than earlier styles. It contained elements of surprise, such as drummers making unheralded accents, vividly described as 'dropping bombs'.

Bop was deliberately uncommercial. Few band uniforms were worn, and any attempt to entertain was much more sly and knowing, much more hip and witty.

There was an influx of 'original' tunes. Usually these were written on the harmonic progression of a favorite standard. The new melody would be composed in the vocabulary of bebop, using mostly eighth notes, with few sustained tones. Thus the music sounded modern, yet

Much has been made of the musical innovations that the bop pioneers brought to jazz. Yet it was not any single development that characterized the new music. Some commentators earnestly cite the flattened fifth (or its compound equivalent the sharpened eleventh), and the interval of the tritone as emblematic of modern jazz, a forties counterpart to the flattened (blues) third of earlier jazz. This merely reveals that the writer has not listened very widely. The flattened fifth had appeared in classical music in the nineteenth century. Chopin's *Mazurka* in B♭, Op. 7, No. 1, is a famous and beautiful example, from 1832. Stravinsky explored tritone relationships in *The Rite of Spring*. In early jazz, sharpened elevenths can be found in Bix Beiderbecke's piano solos from the late twenties onwards, particularly in *In a Mist*. Benny Goodman's *A Smooth One* uses the tritone (flattened fifth) as its opening melodic interval, and Art Tatum used this chromaticism regularly. Even chromatic sideslips had been heard before, notably in the release of *Stompin' at the Savoy*, composed in 1936.

had widely known harmonies on which to improvise. This was helpful in jam sessions, where there was no time to rehearse or learn fresh material. Even this was not a particularly new practice. For example, *Moten Swing*, recorded by the Bennie Moten band in 1932, is based on *You're Driving Me Crazy*.

This method of composition offered a financial advantage. One cannot copyright a chord progression. A musician only had to write his own 'line', based on the chords of a favorite standard, to be able to claim performance royalties. The progression of *Whispering* was used for *Groovin' High, How High the Moon* became *Ornithology*, and *I Got Rhythm* harmonies supported *Anthropology*. At the ends of phrases, and at turnbacks, the harmonic progressions were now more chromatic, introducing notes outside the key. Instead of a diatonic V1-II-V-I turnback (Am7/Dm7/Gm7/C7 in the key of F major), the beboppers would perhaps choose ♭III-♭VI-II-V (A♭m7/D♭7/Gm7/C7) to bring to their performances the color of notes outside the prevailing key.

Therefore, modern jazz did not suddenly appear as a revolutionary style. It evolved. Those assisting in this process of evolution included many who made their names as swing musicians: saxophonists Don Byas and Lester Young, pianists Art Tatum and Nat King Cole, trumpeter Roy Eldridge, bassist Jimmy Blanton and guitarist Charlie Christian.

At the beginning, bop had a rough ride, both from critics and older musicians. Cab Calloway famously told Dizzy Gillespie not to play 'that Chinese music' in his band, while Louis Armstrong was encouraged to perform a modified *Whiffenpoof Song,* renamed *'Boppenpoof Song'*, gently deriding bop. *Down Beat* gave Parker's first album no stars. The new jazz may have been easy to lampoon, but one important characteristic could not be ridiculed: Dizzy Gillespie and Charlie Parker wanted to be treated as artists, not entertainers.

Bebop had more than its fair share of tragic geniuses. Paradoxically, despite his nickname, trumpeter John Birks 'Dizzy' Gillespie was one of the more sober and well-organized of the leading bop figures, harmonically advanced, curious and enquiring about music.

Others had difficulties. Pianist Bud Powell suffered mental problems. Bassist and bandleader Charlie Mingus challenged authority and wrote about it in *Beneath the Underdog*. Pianist and composer Thelonious Monk was misunderstood, widely labeled as weird. Trumpeter Fats Navarro, born 24 September 1923, died of a combination of tuberculosis and narcotics addiction on 7 July 1950, not quite 27. Tenor saxophonist Wardell Gray was found dead in the desert in mysterious circumstances. Richard Twardzik (1931-1955), pianist with Chet Baker, died from a heroin overdose at 24. But the great tragic genius of bebop was Charlie Parker.

Charlie Parker

Beyond all his jazz contemporaries Charlie Parker (1920-1955) was one of the great influential figures of twentieth-century music. Also known as 'Yardbird', 'Yard' or 'Bird', Parker was the prodigiously dissolute genius of the saxophone, worn out and dead at thirty-four. At his best, Parker seemed to throw off melodic ideas like a child's sparkler, dazzling his contemporaries.

Parker influenced a couple of generations of saxophonists. Many alto players developed styles that were grounded in Parker's approach. Cannonball Adderley, Ornette Coleman, Sonny Criss, John Dankworth, Eric Dolphy, Arne Domnérus, Lou Donaldson, Herb Geller, Gigi Gryce, Derek Humble, Peter King, Jackie McLean, Harold McNair, Charles McPherson, Charlie Mariano, James Moody, Lennie Niehaus, Gene Quill, Sonny Stitt, Phil Woods and Leo Wright were among the best. Parker's influence extended to other saxophonists. They included tenorists Albert Ayler, John Coltrane, Stan Getz, Dexter Gordon, Wardell Gray, Joe Farrell, Lucky Thompson and Sonny Rollins. One must also mention baritonist Serge Chaloff, and clarinetist Buddy DeFranco (b. 1923). DeFranco is a brilliant, reliable, long-lived and yet scandalously overlooked jazz musician - at least, in terms of public popularity. Although his brilliance has been recognized in that he has won more magazine polls than any other jazz clarinetist, including twenty *Down Beat* awards, twelve *Playboy* awards and fourteen *Metronome* awards, mysteriously, he has never become a great box office success. [2]

In considering the influence of Charlie Parker it would probably be simpler to list those saxophone contemporaries of Parker whose playing takes an alternative approach. Most notably, these include Paul Desmond, Lee Konitz, Art Pepper and Bud Shank on alto, Warne Marsh on tenor. The complete group of players whose lives Parker changed is huge, far too large to be listed here, embracing brass players and rhythm section players, and from several generations.

Parker was born at 852, Freeman Street, Kansas City, Kansas on 29 August, 1920. His father, Charles Senior, was a pianist and vaudeville singer and, in the account of his wife Addie, a sot.[3] He died of stab wounds in a drunken quarrel when his son was seventeen. According to Doris, Bird's wife from 1948 to 1950, "Charlie's childhood did not ruin Charlie. He had no childhood." [4] Charlie started playing at the age of thirteen, was going on Benzedrine parties at the age of fourteen and was first married at sixteen.[5] By the time he was seventeen he was in New York on hard drugs.

In his earliest recordings, *Honeysuckle Rose* and *Lady be Good,* made with the Jay McShann orchestra in 1941, Parker's virtuosity, trademark tone and rhythmic style are already perceptible. Naturally, the McShann band played in the prevailing swing genre. What we hear in these early recordings is fascinating, but still a long way from the fully formed modern jazz idiom later to be known as bebop. Parker's first small group sessions, recorded in New York in 1944, highlight the difficulties of the rhythm sections in adapting to the new music. The chugging dance-orientated accompaniment sounds prosaic against Parker's extraordinary blues-infused and metrically oblique improvisations.

Parker eventually found a suitable supporting rhythm section for the first recordings made under his own name. Four sides, the Savoy Sessions, were made in November 1945, three months after the surrender of Japan at the end of World War II. His definitive bebop combo turned in a series of masterpieces, *Ko Ko, Billie's Bounce, Thrivin' on a Riff* and *Now's the Time,* the latter one of the great examples of Parker's blues playing. The critics displayed slowness to adapt to the new music. *Down Beat* magazine awarded *Now's the Time* no stars in a review. These recordings featured Dizzy Gillespie and Miles Davis on trumpets, pianist Argonne Thornton, bassist Curley Russell and drummer Max Roach.

Parker was admitted to the Camarillo State Hospital, California, in 1946, because of a nervous breakdown and addiction to heroin and alcohol. Returning to New York in 1947 he formed a quintet with Miles Davis, pianist Duke Jordan, bassist Tommy Potter and drummer Max Roach. The period that followed saw the preservation of some of his best work. Professional recordings were made in studios, and amateur ones made at club performances, parties and concerts.

In 1951, Parker's New York cabaret license was revoked. Withdrawn at the request of the narcotics squad, this barred him from employment in the city's nightclubs. This was the beginning of his decline, though he can still be heard at his best in the famous *Jazz at Massey Hall* recording, made in Toronto in 1953, in the company of Bud Powell, Dizzy Gillespie, Charles Mingus and Max Roach.

In 1953, the death from pneumonia at the age of two of Parker's daughter, Pree, hit him hard. After two attempts at suicide in 1954, he died in 1955, in the Stanhope Hotel, at 995 Fifth Avenue in Manhattan, in the suite of the sister of Lord Rothschild, the Baroness Pannonica de Koenigswarter. In the expert opinion of Frederick J. Spencer, MD, "it is almost immaterial how Charlie Parker died as it was years of unremitting substance abuse that really killed him." [6]

Who influenced Parker? Drummer Kenny Clarke was in no doubt. "We went to listen to Bird at Monroe's for no other reason except that he sounded like Prez. That is, until we found out that he had something of his own to offer." [7] Parker is said to have taken some Lester Young recordings with him to a summer resort job in the Ozark Hills, and 'played them white.' Seventy-eight records were pressed from a brittle shellac, which turned from black to white as the discs wore out. In the days of variable speed record players it was possible to give a convincing demonstration of Young's influence on Parker by playing a Lester Young LP track at 45 rpm instead of 33 rpm. Speeded-up Lester Young tenor solos sound a little like Bird's alto solos, though there is an obliquity about Parker's playing that is absent from accelerated Prez. Perhaps this was what Parker had in mind when he said: "I was crazy about Lester. He played so clean and beautiful. But I wasn't influenced by Lester. Our ideas ran on differently." [8]

Whatever Parker said, Lester Young had a major effect on the alto player. There were other influences. Parker also played and recorded on tenor, though his tenor work in the early 1940s is derivative of Ben Webster and Leon Chu Berry, rather than Prez. If further evidence is needed, remember that Charlie Parker named one of his children Leon, after Berry. Pianist Art Tatum was also important to Parker. As previously mentioned, Bird took a job washing dishes in a restaurant where Tatum appeared in New York, so that he could hear the great pianist at work.

Players who contributed to the experimentation that led to the emergence of bop included tenor saxophonist Don Byas, pianist Nat Cole, trumpeter Roy Eldridge, guitarist Charlie Christian and bassist Jimmy Blanton. Classical music is also sometimes cited when the influences of bebop are listed. Just as the more thoughtful musicians of the 1920s listened to Debussy, Prokofiev and Ravel, some of the progressive musicians of the 1940s listened to Bartók and Stravinsky. Composer Darius Milhaud encouraged Dave Brubeck in playing jazz.[9] Charlie Parker was a friend of the Paris-born composer Edgard Varèse (1883-1965), who had gone to live in America in 1915, and became a US citizen in 1926.

Parker approached the composer for lessons. Varèse said, "He'd come in and exclaim, 'Take me as you would a baby and teach me music. I only write in one voice. I want to have structure. I want to write orchestral scores. I'll give you any amount you wish. I make a lot of money. I'll be your servant. I'm a good cook; I'll cook for you.' He was so dramatic it was funny, but he was sincere." [10]

Why Was Charlie Parker Important?

- Like Louis Armstrong before him, Parker influenced a generation of soloists and changed the course of jazz. He was the player who contributed most to the style of modern jazz known as rebop, bebop, or bop.

- A new virtuosity came to jazz, inspired by Parker's saxophone playing.

- Parker built on Lester Young's use of uneven phrase lengths, with unexpected placement of the beginnings and endings of phrases.

- The chromatic harmony investigated by Art Tatum and others was integrated into Parker's approach, and into the jazz language.

- Bop, in which Parker was the leading figure, saw a new vocabulary of licks emerge, partly created by Dizzy Gillespie, Thelonious Monk, Bud Powell and others, but influenced and inspired by Parker.

- Despite all of the above points, Parker's music is firmly rooted in the jazz tradition, and in the blues.

- Many of the lines Parker wrote, such as *Billie's Bounce, Now's the Time, Donna Lee* and *Ornithology,* have become jazz standards, still played today.

- Rhythm sections were obliged to develop new accompaniment styles to accommodate bebop horn players. They abandoned the chugging dance-orientated approach of the swing bands. Two-in-a-bar bass lines were now rarely heard. Drummers focused more on their cymbals, though the bass drum is still clearly heard, for example in the playing of Max Roach. Pianists supported soloists by stabbing interjections of harmonic support known as comping. Left-hand figures associated with styles such as stride and boogie-woogie were discarded.

- Jazz now moved away from the dance hall and entertainment, to return to being considered as art. It also waned in popularity. Interest in the clarinet declined.

Thelonious Monk

Composer/ pianist Thelonious Sphere Monk (1917-1982) seems to increase in historical importance as the years pass by. He grew up in New York, hearing Willie 'The Lion' Smith and James P. Johnson. He absorbed their stride styles, yet sounded like no other pianist in jazz. Pianists he influenced include Andrew Hill (b.1937), Herbie Nicholls (1919-1963), Cecil Taylor (b.1929) and the British pianist Stan Tracey (b. 1926), known for his long stint as house pianist at Ronnie Scott's club in London.

Monk's compositions, such as *Criss Cross, Epistrophy, Evidence, Misterioso, Off Minor, 'Round Midnight, Straight No Chaser,* and *Well You Needn't,* are still jam session favorites and essential repertoire for the serious jazz musician. Monk's style incorporates angular melodies, use of the whole tone scale, crushed notes, clusters and unexpected notes. Unlike most jazz pianists, his keyboard technique shows little evidence of conventional (classical) schooling. He is a master of rhythmic displacement - the reiteration of short phrases, occurring at a different part of the bar at each repetition. Between 1959 and 1970 Thelonious Monk played regularly with tenor saxophonist Charlie Rouse (1924-1988).

The New Orleans Revival

Now jazz took two paths. The progressives of modern jazz, wearing berets, goatee beards, horn-rimmed spectacles and crepe-soled shoes, ostensibly followed the modernist route that had also been the course of painting, sculpture and classical music. They celebrated the abstract, the surreal, the experimental, the modernist, the hip - or rather the *hep* as it was then. It was a trend which had already begun on 52nd Street in New York, and at Clarke Monroe's Uptown House. Swiftly, not very far in the future, it was to turn to the quest for simplicity, resulting in Miles Davis introducing modes into his performances. But that was later.

Meanwhile, another quest for a return to basics resulted in a very different answer. The impetus came from the traditionalists in San Francisco, London and Paris. These were the duffle-coat-and-corduroy brigade, later to morph into owners of pot bellies, beards and sandals. In those days, when attending university was a privilege of the elite, they were the varsity and art school types, the young 'ban the bomb' campaigners, who wanted to dance to jazz. Their hearts remained with the music of the Hot Fives and Sevens, with singer Bessie Smith, or with the younger New Orleans men like George Lewis and Jim Robinson. This was the revival of traditional New Orleans Jazz.

Revivalists believed that the swing era had taken jazz away from its homely, unpretentious working class origins. To them, jazz was an urban folk music, essentially simple. The new bebop experiments were leading jazz yet further away from its roots, from work song, from informal music making, from uncomplicated music for everyday activities.

Revivalism was an international phenomenon. In America at this time, many people heard their first jazz played by the Dukes of Dixieland, or The Firehouse Five, the latter a band whose members worked by day for the Disney organization. Former Casa Loma trombonist Pee Wee Hunt and his band cut a huge hit record of *12th Street Rag* (1948), in the Dixieland style. In San Francisco, a group of revivalists, the Yerba Buena Jazz Band was active under the leadership of Turk Murphy.

In Australia, the band of Graeme Bell was at the center of the movement. In France, Claude Luter was popular. In London important revivalists included Ken Colyer, Humphrey Lyttelton and Chris Barber.

The revivalists sought out neglected older players. They aimed to recreate performances of simple New Orleans music. Cornet player Bunk Johnson (1889-1949), long out of music, was tracked down. Sidney Bechet's dentist brother, Leonard, made Bunk some teeth, to encourage Bunk to play again. The careers of other older musicians were revived. George Lewis, Jim Robinson - even members of the ODJB - were traced, and approached to perform and record. The revivalists possessed a formidable intensity of purpose. They made a considerable impact on the music scene. In Britain, the trumpet player Ken Colyer (1928-1988) was a leading figure. Through him, the British revival scene led eventually beyond jazz, to one of the biggest changes in the history of twentieth century popular music.

Colyer led a band in London. To study the music in its birthplace, Colyer took a job in the British Merchant Navy. He jumped ship in New Orleans - to be promptly arrested. The remaining musicians of the Colyer band, now led by trombonist and bass player Chris Barber (b.1930), went on to enjoy enduring commercial success from the middle 1950s. They even had a hit record in America, a simple melodic version of the Sidney Bechet tune *Petite Fleur,* in a small group version played by clarinetist Monty Sunshine.

Where the Beatles Began

Then came the biggest, but indirect, impact of the revivalists. Chris Barber's main sideshow was the inclusion of a skiffle group within the band. This featured the band's banjoist, Lonnie Donegan (1931-2002), singing and playing guitar, supported by a second guitar, double bass and drums. Skiffle took the concept of simplicity to the maximum. Some British skiffle groups (not Barber's) featured a blown jug as a wind bass, a tea chest with a broom handle as a string bass, a kazoo as a melody instrument, and spoons, bones and washboard as supplementary percussion.

The skiffle movement, and Lonnie Donegan's uncomplicated, even corny, hit records, inspired a generation of young amateur players. Skiffle created an opportunity to perform in public with a minimum of skill, with amateur musicians playing their own accompaniment to songs which were usually adapted from folk material or self-composed. The harmonies were basic, frequently a blues or similar, calling for a handful of chords. Players talked of the 'three chord trick', alluding to the three primary triads, chords one, four and five. Usually that was all that was needed, spawning the famous instruction: "Here's a chord. Here's another chord. Now form a band."

Later, the Beatles developed out of a Liverpool skiffle group, the Quarrymen. Many other British rock musicians, from Pete Townsend of The Who to Charlie Watts of the Rolling Stones, acknowledge the place of skiffle in their formative years. Again, jazz had an important influence on popular music, possibly its greatest effect of all.

In one respect the revivalists created a distorted version of history. Much of the music that came out of the revival movement was played by instrumentalists who were amateurs. They were only concerned with recreating the jazz that they had heard on record. What they overlooked, or did not deem important, was the great respect for musicianship and technical skill that had been part of the musical culture in New Orleans at the time of the birth of jazz.

Clarinetist Albert Nicholas (1900-1973) has spoken of his childhood growing up in New Orleans, of listening to a wide variety of music, including recordings of Italian opera. He recounts the thoroughness of the private lessons given by such important teachers as clarinetist Lorenzo Tio. Scales were learned in all keys. The ability to read music at sight was cultivated, as was the ability to transpose at sight.

However, this was not true of all the New Orleans musicians. On their own testimony, four of the five members of the ODJB were unable to read music. [11] Of his own contemporaries, clarinetist Paul Barnes said: "We played ragtime, but we couldn't read. And we played a different ragtime from those reading musicians who actually played it . . . most of the traditional men, they couldn't read... They had great men that could play those instruments who couldn't read, but who were more familiar with their instrument than the men that read. But they weren't considered. Only the people that read music were considered great musicians. Of course, some of the others were great, as I've told you, but they wouldn't give them any art." [12]

Many of the revivalists could not read music. Some steadfastly refused to learn the names of the notes on their instruments, or named them wrongly, treating a transposing instrument such as the Bb clarinet as a concert pitch instrument. They identified the notes by the sounds they made rather than attempting to understand the simple concept of transposition. Many revival bands played only in two or three keys, usually Bb, C and F, regarded as the easiest keys for technically weak wind players. Some clung to the view that this was an important part of playing with authenticity. They believed that learning to read music, or to understand the rudiments of harmony or music terminology, would damage their playing in some way.

The opposite was the case. Many of these endearingly enthusiastic autodidacts consigned themselves to a lifetime of restricted musical competence, happy to recreate a limited version of early New Orleans jazz. At least they were making music, from the heart. Who is to say they were mistaken?

One engaging quality of the New Orleans revival is the loyalty of the players. Even today, revivalist New Orleans jazz can be heard in every large city in the western world, and even in Japan. This devotion is epitomized by film actor, writer and director Woody Allen (b.1935). An amateur clarinetist in a New York based New Orleans style band, and an avid enthusiast, Woody even skipped the 1978 Oscar ceremony so that he could play jazz in a Manhattan bar. That night his film *Annie Hall* was awarded best picture and best screenplay honors in Los Angeles, while he remained in New York to play a clarinet gig.

Birth of the Cool

Several jazz movements followed swiftly in the wake of bop and revivalism. In quick succession came cool jazz, hard bop, West Coast jazz and Third Stream jazz. At this time - the late 1940s - the beginnings of *free jazz* were also first heard. Each genre did not thrust aside its forerunner. Throughout jazz history, every new style runs alongside its predecessors, so that today one can hear a wide variety of jazz types, all coexisting.

Miles Davis was only nineteen years old when Charlie Parker offered him the job with Parker's combo at the Three Deuces on 52nd Street. From 1945 until 1947 Davis worked and recorded with Parker. Billy Eckstine's observation that Miles 'sounded terrible' (see p. 131) is borne out by the evidence of some of these early recordings with Parker, where he exhibits limited technique, small range, inaccurate intonation and a tendency to fluff notes. However, eventually Miles worked toward a style that was entirely his own. He developed a beautiful personal sound, with an economy of notes and great lyricism.

Davis brought his flair for texture and color to various innovative projects, beginning with the nine-piece band which he led for a two week engagement in 1948 at the Royal Roost Club in New York. This was the famous 'Birth of the Cool' band. Thus, the first appearance of cool jazz can be dated exactly.

The personnel included Lee Konitz, John Lewis, Gerry Mulligan and Kai Winding. Gil Evans (1912-1988), who was the senior member of the band, played a pivotal role behind the scenes. He wrote some of the arrangements, helped by Lewis, but Gerry Mulligan wrote the majority, almost half of the pieces recorded. [13] The musicians were young, Davis only twenty-three. They hung out together at Evans's basement apartment behind a Chinese laundry on W55[th] Street, near Fifth Avenue. Their idea was to create a small band that emulated the various bands of Claude Thornhill (1909-1965) in the matter of instrumentation. Thornhill had been a successful swing era arranger, at least one of his arrangements having been heard on the Benny Goodman Carnegie Hall concert of 1938. Of the Thornhill band of 1941 Gunther Schuller wrote: "Thornhill's own originals...emphasized clarinet and horn sonorities...usually set in sustained backgrounds in the middle and low registers in slow tempos: a soft carpet of sound over which Thornhill could weave his famous 'one finger' melodies and spellbinding embroideries. It was an irresistible sonoric combination...its effect was often quite magical." [14] The Davis nonet had no guitar, no tenor saxophone, no clarinet (though the Thornhill band had at one point no less than seven clarinets), and introduced the French horn to jazz instrumentation.

"That was a result of these composers getting together, Gerry Mulligan, John Lewis, Gil Evans, Johnny Carisi and George Russell. It was a chamber music group that the composers had conceived of, a reduced Claude Thornhill band, basically, with a French horn, and a tuba - Claude had two French horns and a tuba...Miles was the main voice, and he could get the gigs. He got one record date and one week's gig, that was the history of that band! ...But it was a composer's band basically. The birth of the cool was more Lester Young, and Tristano and the improvisers. But you've got to have a descriptive phrase, and that was a good one." [15]

The nonet had an influence far beyond the few people that heard it perform live, for the band only worked for a fortnight, in 1948. The nonet was recorded in 1949 and 1950, and the tracks were later issued as *The Birth of the Cool* in 1957.

Lee Konitz (b. 1927) objected to the word 'cool' as a description of his style. The British journalist Andy Hamilton explained: "The group of young musicians around Tristano was early on described as the Cool School, but 'cool' in this sense is a term which Konitz dislikes. The Tristano School is portrayed as opposed to bebop when in fact there were common roots in the work of Lester Young, and its music had an intensity just as real for being more subtly expressed. Konitz still favors Tristano's distinction between feeling, which is necessary, and emotion - really 'emoting' - which is a distraction from the real music." [16]

"I feel that in a positive way that's a great description. The negative connotation is what was really used on us, as white unpassionate players. I didn't appreciate that. If you're talking about cool, you're talking about Louis Armstrong, Lester Young, Charlie Parker - all the people who could really play unaffected music. When it became affected, to me, trying to be emotional, trying to be funky, trying to be something other than natural, then it became hot. But the real music was cool." [17]

To further confuse the issue, there are those who assert that cool jazz had its origins long before, in the 1920s. They believe that Jelly Roll Morton, Arthur Whetsol, Joe Smith, Bix Beiderbecke and Miff Mole were cool players in all but name.

The cool movement has not been without its critics. Stanley Crouch, in an article entitled 'On the Corner: The Sell-out of Miles Davis,' said that, "Heard now, the nonet recordings seem like little more than primers for television writing...another attempt to marry jazz to European devices." [18] To make his point about the sell-out of Davis, Crouch is conveniently forgetting that the nonet came before the nonet-style television writing. Television was in its infancy in 1948.

The label 'cool' persisted. Even today it is still used in pop music, pop culture and advertising, most of its users unaware that it original-ly described a type of modern jazz of the late 1940s and early 1950s.

In the jazz sense it describes music that is less demonstrative than bop, the players tending to use light instrumental tone with very little vibrato, making a feature of linear arrangements with counterpoint. Now the rhythm guitar and clarinet were dropped. The vibraphone, flugelhorn and flute appeared more frequently.

The LP Arrives

The twelve inch vinyl long playing record (LP) was introduced to the American market in 1948. The LP was launched in Europe later. Whilst there was ever a limit on the length of a recording, the distinc-tion between performance and recording had been clear. Once magnetic wire, later tape, was used, many new possibilities were available. Long performances, with extended improvisations, could be recorded. Blemishes could be removed. It was but a small step to multitrack recording.

West Coast Jazz

The most important subcategory of cool is West Coast Jazz. This is the music played by schooled white Californian jazz musicians, based in San Francisco and Los Angeles. West Coast style combos included the Gerry Mulligan Quartet, the Dave Brubeck Quartet, Shorty Rogers and his Giants, the Modern Jazz Quartet, Lennie Niehaus Octet, the Dave Pell Octet, the George Shearing Quintet, the Marty Paich Dektette, and the Chico Hamilton Quintet.

The big bands of Woody Herman and Stan Kenton were also comprised largely of West Coast players. Shorty Rogers (1924-1994) is a particularly interesting figure, now overlooked. An arranger, composer and bandleader, he was one of the first to take up the flugelhorn, and influenced Stravinsky to call for the instrument in *Threni,* a religious choral work written in 1957-8 (ref. *Conversations*). Rogers was a pioneer of experiments with bitonality, twelve-tone technique in jazz, and improvising on modes. Not all of the music was cool, not all of the performers were white. Other musicians active in California during this period included tenorists Dexter Gordon, Teddy Edwards, Wardell Gray and Harold Land, bassist Curtis Counce, and a number of musicians associated with The Lighthouse, a club on Hermosa beach, California.

The Quartet of Gerry Mulligan (1927-1996) was pianoless, but it was not the first pianoless group in modern jazz. That distinction belongs to an early bebop band led by Dizzy Gillespie on 52nd Street in 1943. [19] However, where bop had struggled to find an audience, some West Coast

Top: Original Dixieland Jazz Band. Bottom: Adrian Rollini. Photos from the Institute of Jazz Studies at Rutgers University, Newark, New Jersey.

Top: Hoagy Carmichael and Duke Ellington. Photo from the Institute of Jazz Studies at Rutgers University, Newark, New Jersey. Bottom: Billie Holiday. Photo from Star Line Productions.

Top: Erroll Garner.
Bottom: Count Basie
drinking.
Photos from the Institute
of Jazz Studies at
Rutgers University,
Newark, New Jersey.

Top: Count Basie Band in 1938, with Lester Young in the saxophone section, seated furthest from Basie.
Bottom: Charlie Parker. Photos from the Institute of Jazz Studies at Rutgers University, Newark, New Jersey.

Collection of matchbook covers.

Top: Miles Davis with Gil Evans. In the background is record producer Teo Macero. Photo by Don Huntstein. Courtesy of Columbia Records. Bottom: Louis Armstrong at Leeds Airport, England, in 1968, meeting Enrico Tomasso. Enrico's father is pictured with them. Photo from Gilloon Agency.

*Michael Brecker.
Photo by Michael
Piazza.*

John Abercrombie. Photo by Howard Goodman / ECM Records.

Jan Garbarek. Photo by Roberto Masotti / ECM Records.

Dave Holland.
Photo by
Laurence Labat /
ECM Records.

Top: Kenny Wheeler. Photo by ECM Records. Bottom: Keith Jarrett. Photo by Patrick Hinely Work / ECM Records.

musicians enjoyed commercial success almost without seeking it. The formative years of Dave Brubeck (b. 1920) at Mills College in California saw the pianist organizing an octet and studying with the French composer Darius Milhaud. Later, Brubeck ran a successful quartet with the alto saxophonist Paul Desmond (1924-1977).

In 1954, Dave Brubeck was the first jazz musician to appear on the cover of the prestigious *Time* magazine, being accorded that honor even before Duke Ellington. In 1959 Brubeck had an unexpected top forty success with Paul Desmond's composition *Take Five,* a simple piece in five-four time that included a lengthy drum solo. Not the sort of composition one would have created if asked to come up with a hit record, nevertheless it was the first jazz instrumental piece to sell a million copies. The 1959 Brubeck Quartet album *Time Out* was the first jazz LP to sell a million.

British born George Shearing had an international career, based on the attractive sound of his quintet. The group's playing of Shearing's own *Lullaby of Birdland,* composed in 1952, was a hit which became a jazz standard. George Shearing devised his own instantly recognizable sound, where 'locked hands' piano phrased the melody precisely between the vibraphone and guitar. They doubled the melody in octaves, the piano sandwiched the harmony between. Shearing is an excellent pianist, with a phenomenal memory and brilliant command of chromatic harmony. He is too frequently undervalued by commentators.

Important West Coast saxophonists include altoists Buddy Collette, Herb Geller, Lennie Niehaus, Art Pepper, Bud Shank, tenorists Bob Cooper, Jimmy Guiffre, Bill Holman, Richie Kamuca, Jack Montrose, Dave Pell, Bill Perkins and Zoot Sims. Two influential baritone saxophonists are Bob Gordon and Gerry Mulligan. Trumpeters are Chet (Chesney) Baker, Conte Candoli, Maynard Ferguson, Shorty Rogers,

Jack Sheldon and Stu Williamson. Prominent West Coast trombonists are Milt Bernhart, Bob Brookmeyer, Bob Enevoldsen and Frank Rosolino. John Graas, French horn, must also be mentioned.

West Coast style pianists include Russ Freeman, Hampton Hawes, Pete Jolly, Marty Paich, André Previn (who made an impressive Art Tatum-inspired recording at the age of 16), and Claude Williamson. Other prominent cool musicians were saxophonists Serge Chaloff, Lee Konitz, Warne Marsh, Stan Getz, Paul Horn, Gene Quill and Paul Quinichette (the 'Vice-Prez'), and trombonists J. J. Johnson and Kai Winding.

Bassists Red Callender, Carson Smith, Leroy Vinnegar, Red Mitchell, Monty Budwig, Joe Mondragon, Howard Rumsey and Curtis Counce should be mentioned. Drummers included Larry Bunker, Chico Hamilton, Stan Levey, Shelly Manne and Mel Lewis.

Singers Blossom Dearie, Lena Horne, Cleo Laine, Peggy Lee, Carmen McCrae, Dinah Washington, Joe Williams and Nancy Wilson were all active at this time. They were not associated with one particular style of jazz. In contrast, Mel Tormé (1925-1999), though born in Chicago, was always associated with West Coast jazz. He had appeared in vaudeville from an early age, singing and playing the baritone ukulele, an instrument that he continued to bring on stage until the 1960s. A more than competent drummer and pianist, he was a good enough arranger to be able to write his own effective big band orchestrations. Along with Ella Fitzgerald, Louis Armstrong, Anita O'Day, and very few others, Tormé - known as 'the Velvet Fog' - was a most convincing scat singer. Scatting may be skillful; it can certainly be entertaining; it may be what many young singers aspire to do. But emotional contact with listeners is what endures. Tony Scott summed it up: "With a singer like Ella, when she sings 'my man has left me,' you think the guy's going down the street for a loaf of bread. But when

Lady [Billie Holiday] sings it, man, you see the bags are packed, the cat's going down the street, and you know he ain't never coming back." [20]

References

1. Morgenstern, D., 'Death of 52nd St.', 1962,
    http://www.allaboutjazz.com/journalists/morgenstern2.htm
2. Zammarch, F. and Mas, S., *A Life in the Golden Age of Jazz* (Seattle: Parkside Publications, 2002), p. 299.
3. Reisner, R., *Bird, The Legend of Charlie Parker* (London: MacGibbon and Kee, 1962), p. 159.
4. Ibid., p. 173.
5. Ibid., p. 158.
6. Spencer, F. J., *Jazz and Death* (University of Mississippi Press, 2002), p.139.
7. Shapiro, N. and Hentoff, N., op. cit., p.354.
8. Ibid., p. 355.
9. Ibid., p. 392.
10. Reisner, R., op.cit., pp. 229, 230.
11. Rust, B., op. cit., p.16.
12. Jones, M., op. cit., pp.3, 4.
13. Gioia, T., *West Coast Jazz* (University of California Press, 1998), p.177.
14. Schuller, G., *The Swing Era* (OUP, 1989), p. 756.
15. Hamilton, A., 'Intuition and Digression', *Jazz Review*, Issue 16, December 2000, p. 14.
16. Ibid., p.12.
17. Ibid., p.13.
18. Crouch, S., *The All-American Skin Game* (Pantheon, 1995), p. 39.
19. Shapiro, N. and Hentoff, N., op. cit., p.367.
20. Scott, T., 'Comparing Ella Fitzgerald and Billie Holiday', in Nat Hentoff's *Jazz Times*, Internet edition, July 2000.

7. Jazz on a Summer's Day

It is 1958. President Eisenhower is serving his second term in the White House. On a summer's day we are on the east coast between New York and Boston, at Newport, Rhode Island.

Newport has long been associated with North America's rich. Jacqueline Bouvier, John F. Kennedy's First Lady, grew up here. During the nineteenth century, many of the truly wealthy built vacation homes on the island. They were the Astors, the Vanderbilts, George Bancroft the secretary of the Navy, and a dozen other prosperous folk. They called their summer dwellings 'cottages', a massive understatement, an affectation. More akin to stately homes or castles, each cost several million dollars, each strove to outdo its neighbor. Marble was imported from Italy, soil from England. Horses slept on linen, other pets ate caviar.

These palaces - there is no better word to describe them - sit side by side in their own grounds along The Avenue in Newport. In 1958 they are too expensive, too lavish, for any contemporary individual to want them. The Avenue elite are long gone. The cottages are now open to tourists and film crews. *The Great Gatsby,* a movie of Scott Fitzgerald's 1920s novel, will be filmed here in 1974.

Out in Narragansett Bay there are hundreds of sailing boats. Newport is a leading yachting center. This summer the America's Cup Trials take place here. There is a delicious impertinence about holding one of the world's great jazz festivals in this place. It shares that characteristic with the first jazz concert in Carnegie Hall, back in 1938, twenty years ago.

The Newport Jazz Festival started in 1954, the idea of two local jazz lovers, Elaine and Louis Lorillard. Impresario George Wein made it happen. Wein decided that all styles of jazz should be represented. Therefore, the first Festival featured Eddie Condon's Chicagoans, Dizzy Gillespie, Count Basie, Stan Kenton, Dave Brubeck, Louis Armstrong, Pee Wee Russell and Stan Getz. It was a success.

The next year, 1955, Miles Davis appeared. In 1956 the Duke Ellington band played here, giving an historic performance to a wildly enthusiastic audience. Their definitive *Diminuendo and Crescendo in Blue* had Paul Gonsalves on tenor saxophone playing the solo of a lifetime, twenty-seven choruses, with the crowd cheering every one. The band romped through four encores. The recording of the concert sold more copies than any other record Duke made. For decades it was sold with the sound balance badly adjusted, Gonsalves's saxophone off-mike. Only far into the future, in the late 1990s, was the recording corrected.

After a mere four years the Newport Festival is famous, with a reputation for presenting the leading modernists. Since rock 'n' roll burst onto the scene a couple of years ago there has been much interest in singers and the guitar. This year at Newport we are going to hear Chuck Berry and gospel singer Mahalia Jackson. But it is the jazz that we have come to enjoy.

Of course, we have LPs or 78s of many of the artists; both types of phonograph records exist. More prosperous enthusiasts also have home tape recorders running quarter-inch tape. Little jazz is heard on the radio, and many of us never get to see our jazz favorites unless they tour near to where we live. Most homes now have a black and white television. There are few jazz programs on TV.

Here at Newport this July the enthusiastic audience is mostly aged between the late teens and late thirties. The four days of the Festival include the Jimmy Guiffre Three (with Bob Brookmeyer and Jim Hall, in an unforgettable performance of *The Train and the River)*, the Thelonious Monk Trio with Henry Grimes and Roy Haynes, the Miles Davis Quintet, Sonny Stitt and Sal Salvador, Lester Young, Tony Scott with Jimmy Knepper, Lee Konitz, the Horace Silver Quintet, Anita O'Day scatting on the ever-doubling-tempo arrangement of *Tea for Two,* Sonny Rollins, the George Shearing Quintet, the Gerry Mulligan Quartet, Big Maybelle Smith, Willie 'The Lion' Smith, Chuck Berry, the Chico Hamilton Quintet, the Louis Armstrong All Stars with Jack Teagarden, Dinah Washington and Mahalia Jackson. The musicians play outdoors on temporary stages. Listeners sit on folding chairs.

A documentary film shot during the 1958 Newport Festival will be issued in 1959. Called *Jazz on a Summer's Day,* it will prove to be a classic. Later to be reissued on video tape and DVD, it will still be viewed with pleasure half a century later.

Duke Ellington

If you are seeking evidence that jazz can arouse an audience to wild appreciation, equivalent to the kind of response usually encountered at a football or baseball match, a major rock concert, or popular opera in a small Italian town, you need look no further than those recordings made by the Ellington band at the Newport Festival in 1956. Harry Carney playing *Sophisticated Lady,* Johnny Hodges performing *I Got It Bad and That Ain't Good,* Sam Woodyard soloing on Louie Bellson's *Skin Deep,* as well as the band with their theme tune, Strayhorn's *Take the A Train,* were all performances of a lifetime. The listeners knew they were witnessing something special. Fortunately, all of this is preserved on CD. And of course, it includes Paul Gonsalves's version of *Diminuendo and Crescendo in Blue.*

In presenting the unfolding of jazz history in chronological order, there is no obvious point at which to discuss Edward Kennedy 'Duke' Ellington (1899-1974). Pianist and bandleader, Duke was the first genuine jazz composer of truly international status, with a productivity that dazzles in quantity and quality. "The number of Ellington's compositions has been variously estimated in the jazz and lay press to be anywhere between 1,000 and 5,000...around 750 works are by Ellington alone, 200 are collaborations with his own musicians (half of these with Billy Strayhorn), and 50 are collaborations with others. Owing to the astonishing lack of care and respect afforded to Ellington's original manuscripts during and after his life, a definitive census of his works may never be accurately accomplished. It is not difficult to calculate that by normal standards Ellington the composer was outstandingly prolific. Over fifty years he and his collaborators produced twenty compositions each year, or one about every eighteen days; as for the compositions that Ellington wrote himself, these average out to one every twenty-four days."[1]

Born in Washington in 1899, Duke came to New York in 1923. He began as a stride pianist. "I got my first break when I was about seventeen, down in Washington, and Louis Thomas sent for me to play piano one night," he said. "Thomas was the leader of a society band... I was to get a chance to play in his third band on the condition that I would learn to play the *Siren Song* well enough to perform it that night. I spent the whole day learning the tune. When I arrived on the job I found that the band was a legitimate one, they wouldn't play any 'jumps'. The musicians started talking to me about correct chords, and I knew that in a few minutes I'd be sunk. Then somebody requested the

Siren Song, and in great relief I started plunking out the number. I'd often watched Luckey Roberts who had come down from New York to play the Howard Theater. He had a flashy style, and a trick of throwing his hands away from the piano. It occurred to me that I might try doing what he did. Before I knew it the kids around the stand were screaming with delight and clapping for more. In two minutes the flashy hands had earned me a reputation, and after that I was all set. I got a hunch about having my own band."

Ellington's competition, struggle and scheming did not end there. "For a long time I had been rehearsing a riff to make the piano sound like Jimmy Johnson [James P. Johnson]. Everybody was trying to sound like the *Carolina Shout* that Jimmy had made on a player-piano roll. I got it down by slowing up the roll. I had it so close that when Jimmy came to town to play one night, they made me get up on the stage to cut him. I took him out that night for a tour of the Southwest district, and I stayed up until ten a.m. listening to him. All at once it looked like the big break had arrived. Wilbur Sweatman sent down from New York...But when we got there we found out that [he's got] the work that wasn't so good...Sweatman performed every night with his three clarinets in his mouth at one time." [2]

From 1924 Duke was playing in Harlem. He was also on Broadway with Elmer Snowden's band, the Washingtonians. That year Ellington took over as leader. During the next three years the band grew to a ten-piece that featured Bubber Miley (trumpet), Joe 'Tricky Sam' Nanton (trombone), Harry Carney (baritone saxophone), Rudy Jackson (clarinet and tenor saxophone) and Wellman Braud (double bass). The band's early recordings included *Black and Tan Fantasy* and *East St Louis Toodle-oo*, the band's signature tune between 1926 and 1941.

Ellington was recording with his band by the late twenties. In 1927 the band began its legendary stay at the Cotton Club. "We opened up at the Cotton Club, December fourth, in 1927. Jimmy McHugh and Dorothy Fields had scored the show, and Jimmy had been instrumental in getting us the booking. Clarence Robinson and Johnny Vigal were the producers, and the big tunes were *Dancemania* and *Jazzmania*. Later on we played the same show in the Lafayette and Standard Theaters, and these originated the type of entertainment featured at the Apollo today. We were broadcasting at 5 p.m. every day over WHN. Then we really got a break. Columbia sent Ted Husing down to see about putting the band on the air. He got everything settled, and went right to work announcing our programs. He did such a terrific job that our band soon became widely known. By that time, we had twelve men in the band. Bubber and Artie were the trumpets...Johnny Hodges was still with Chick Webb, but we had Toby and Rudy Jackson, and we'd just hired Carney. Carney was only a kid at the time, and we had to tell him everything. He wanted to know what the money was, and when we told him seventy-five dollars, he could hardly credit his ears. By then we were recording almost every day, and for all the labels. We used a dozen different names." [3]

By the thirties Duke Ellington was already regarded as an important contributor to jazz history. He and his band took part in the Benny Goodman Carnegie Hall Concert in 1938, though most would say that his finest moments came in the late 1950s, when Duke and his band played at Newport.

He wrote incessantly, sometimes at great speed. *Solitude* was said to have been composed in twenty minutes. *Black and Tan Fantasy* was rumored to have been written in a taxi driving through Central Park.

"The music's mostly written down, because it saves time," Duke said. "It's written down if it's only a basis for a change. There's no set system. Most times I write it and arrange it. Sometimes I write it and the band and I collaborate on the arrangement. Sometimes Billy Strayhorn, my staff arranger, does the arrangement. When we're all working together, a guy may have an idea and he plays it on his horn. Another guy may add to it and make something out of it. Someone may

> Ellington's later work is characterized by his interest in the reed section. Its five members were together as a team longer than any other in jazz history. [4] A favorite orchestration device was to position the baritone not at the bottom of the section, but as the second voice from the bottom. There are four actual notes in the chord, but the bottom (or fifth) voice, doubling the lead alto, is given to the tenor, with Carney's baritone *above* the tenor. Ellington had his players switch parts at rehearsals and recording sessions. "The warm effect imparted to the ensemble by placing the baritone within, rather than at the bottom of the section [was] may be one of the effects that Ellington sought." [5] Of course, Carney's baritone sounds like no other saxophone in jazz. That is the important part of the secret.

play a riff and ask, 'How do you like this?' The trumpets may try something together and say, 'Listen to this.' There may be a difference of opinion on what kind of mute to use. Someone may advocate extending a note or cutting it off. The sax section may want to put an additional smear on it..." [6]

The strength of Ellington as an orchestrator lies in the special musicians for whom he wrote. He was quick to exploit the unusual timbres around him. He wrote for Harry Carney's baritone saxophone, Lawrence Brown's trombone, Johnny Hodges's alto, Juan Tizol's trombone.

It is the detail, the minutiae of Ellington's scoring, that is significant. André Previn, a masterly composer and orchestrator himself, summed up the Ellington effect excellently: "You know, Stan Kenton can stand in front of a thousand fiddles and a thousand brass and make a dramatic gesture, and every studio arranger can nod his head and say, 'Oh, yes, that's done like this.' But Duke merely lifts his finger, three horns make a sound, and I don't know what it is." [7]

Why Was Duke Ellington Important?

* He is the most prolific composer in jazz, producing work of high quality in high quantity.

* He composed, or co-composed, many melodies that have become jazz standards, including: *Caravan, C Jam Blues, Cottontail, Creole Love Call, Do Nothing 'Till You Hear From Me, I Let a Song Go Out of My Heart, In a Mellotone, In a Sentimental Mood, It Don't Mean a Thing If It Ain't Got That Swing, Mood Indigo, Prelude to a Kiss, Rockin' in Rhythm, Satin Doll, Solitude, Sophisticated Lady,* and others, a total of around one thousand pieces.

* He pioneered the use of lengthy compositions in jazz, including many suites and religious works.

* He led his band, an influential large ensemble featuring several major players and which served as his workshop, for nearly fifty years, from the early 1920s until he died in 1974.

Several devices of orchestration were introduced by Duke. The use of wordless vocals - Adelaide Hall in the 1927 *Creole Love Call* - was an Ellington innovation, as was the technique of voicing across sections. His 'jungle' style emphasized the combination of plunger mute and growl on brass instruments, heard in the playing of Bubber Miley, Cootie Williams and Joe 'Tricky Sam' Nanton.

Third Stream Jazz

From the first days of recorded jazz there had been attempts to combine it with classical music. In the twenties, Bix Beiderbecke and others had expressed admiration for the work of Ravel, Debussy, Delius and Eastwood Lane (see p.52). Paul Whiteman, the bandleader who ran a large ensemble with conspicuous success throughout the inter-war years, whose career and contribution to twentieth century music awaits an overdue re-evaluation, had commissioned *Rhapsody in Blue* from George Gershwin. It was performed in New York's Aeolian Hall in 1924, with Gershwin as soloist (see p.62).

In the thirties, Artie Shaw had experimented with the use of a string quartet. At around the same time, Benny Goodman had begun a courtship with classical music that was to endure until he died in 1986. With Leonard Bernstein at the piano, Goodman had premiered Poulenc's *Clarinet Sonata* in 1963. Goodman's efforts would result in a profusion of commissioned works, from Malcolm Arnold, Bela Bartók, Aaron Copland, Morton Gould, Paul Hindemith and others. The Woody Herman band gave the first performance of Igor Stravinsky's *Ebony Concerto* in 1945. Duke Ellington and John Lewis utilized classical techniques in their jazz writing during the 1940s. Beginning in the 1950s, there were many such cross-references.

Numerous jazz musicians cite classical music as an important part of their listening. Duke Ellington started with classical music. When interviewed by the influential Belgian critic Robert Goffin, in 1946, he said, "I'd take Ravel's *Daphnis and Chloe;* Delius' *In a Summer Garden;* Debussy's *La Mer* and *Afternoon of a Faun;* and the *Planets Suite* [Holst] . . . ." [8] The connections have been there all along.

Classical music supplied much of the material from which many jazz performances and compositions have been spun, from the European music that gave raw material for *Tiger Rag* to the medieval music upon which the Norwegian saxophonist Jan Garbarek based his *Officium* recording. Numerous celebrated pianists of jazz had a grounding in classical music. The line that links Oscar Peterson and Art Tatum goes straight back to Franz Liszt. Several others - Bill Evans, Keith Jarrett, George Shearing, Teddy Wilson - have a technical facility that speaks of an education in the classical repertoire.

The expression *Third Stream* was coined by the historian Gunther Schuller, in an address at Brandeis University, in Boston, Massachusetts, in 1957. It was originally used to describe a style that fused basic elements of jazz and Western art music. In many jazz histories you will not see Third Stream mentioned. Schuller himself admits that the movement has "attracted much controversy and has often erroneously been allied with the symphonic jazz movement of the 1920s." [9] However, the significant difference is that the symphonic jazz movement first emerged in the 1920s, before Third Stream jazz was identified and defined. Although it displayed an awareness of American song and dance, symphonic jazz lacked the crucial element of improvisation.

Schuller names several pieces and composers that can be associated with the Third Stream movement. Those that date from the time of Schuller's first introduction of the term include Milton Babbitt's *All*

Set, on the Brandeis Festival album *Modern Jazz Concert* of 1957, Bill Russo's *An Image of Man,* on the recording *Lee Konitz with Strings,* of 1958, and Schuller's own *Concertino for Jazz Quartet and Orchestra,* on *Modern Jazz Quartet and Orchestra,* of 1960. [10] Third Stream did not appear simultaneously with Schuller's invention of its name. As ever, in all of the arts, historical schools or movements always exist before they are labeled.

Evidence of Third Stream thinking came from Gil Evans, Stan Kenton, Charles Mingus, George Russell and Gunther Schuller. Trumpeter, composer and arranger Don Ellis (1934 - 1978) took the process a step further during the 60s and 70s, with his intriguing big band. The music that influenced Ellis ranged from Balinese gamelan to electronics, and included most of the territory in between.

Ultimately, Third Stream proved not to be the way forward for jazz. Writer Simon Adams summed up the matter perfectly: "Like most life forms that live in the middle of the road, it suffered the ultimate penalty, soon run over by heavier musical traffic passing in either direction." [11]

Stan Getz

One of the great soloists of this period was tenor saxophonist Stan Getz (1927-1991), who was a working musician in Jack Teagarden's band by the time he was sixteen. He joined Stan Kenton in 1944, played with Jimmy Dorsey in 1945 and with Benny Goodman in 1945-46. He was part of Woody Herman's Second Herd from 1947 to 1949, one of the first members of the so-called 'Four Brothers' saxophone section, which included saxophonists Zoot Sims, Serge Chaloff and Herbie Steward. With Herman, in 1948 Getz made the acclaimed recording of *Summer Sequence,* a suite by composer and arranger Ralph Burns (1922-2001), with the beautiful ballad *Early Autumn.*

Getz's worldwide success came with his recordings of the 1960s. With Brazilian composer Antonio Carlos Jobim and singers João and Astrud Gilberto, bossa nova - a mix of Brazilian music and jazz - became popular. Getz recorded *Desafinado*, with guitarist Charlie Byrd, in 1962. His version of *The Girl from Ipanema* in 1963 became one of the best selling records in jazz history. Getz had a distinctive, light, tone; he possessed the ability both to express himself wistfully on a ballad, yet swing aggressively in a jam session. One of the strengths of the saxophonist's style was that he tended to avoid the licks and clichés of the era. Later, pianist Chick Corea and vibraphone player Gary Burton worked regularly with Getz.

Hard bop, as its name implies, is a development of bop. They stem from similar influences. To the uninitiated they sound alike. Hard bop emerged in the 50s, at around the same time as cool jazz. Cool jazz was associated with white Californian musicians, though not exclusively so. Hard bop was more typically played by musicians from Detroit, Philadelphia and the East Coast. West Coast clearly grew from the *Birth of the Cool*. Hard bop favored more complex arrangements, combos up to octet and dektette, use of counterpoint, with instruments not before featured at the forefront of jazz. Light instrumental tones were preferred. Inspirational models from previous jazz eras were Lester Young, Charlie Christian and even Bix Beiderbecke.

Both hard bop and cool jazz can be described as couth, kempt and shevelled versions of bebop. Hard bop was typically performed in small combos, usually with more than one front line instrument (the tenor saxophone featured heavily), the musicians playing arrangements with organized introductions, simple, often linear, backings behind soloists, bridge passages and codas. Pianist Horace Silver (b. 1928) was an important figure in hard bop, leading a series of quintets with trumpet and tenor saxophone front line, the two instruments voiced characteristically in intervals a fourth or a fifth apart. His compositions *Doodlin', Sister Sadie, The Preacher, Song For My Father* and *Filthy McNasty* were to become favorites of the period, breaking away from the bop practice of using chord progressions from standards. In a period rich with good trumpeters, Clifford Brown (1930-1956) had fluency, and a beautiful, unmistakable tone. He was truly outstanding.

Hard bop favored a more virile instrumental tone, simpler arrangements with little counterpoint, and a more driving solo style. Examples of hard bop combos are those of Art Blakey, Benny Golson, the Clifford Brown- Max Roach Quintet, the Cannonball Adderley Quintet and the J. J. Johnson-Kai Winding Quintet, with its front line of two trombones.

Other prominent players in the style included Kenny Dorham, Blue Mitchell, Donald Byrd, Art Farmer, Lee Morgan, Freddie Hubbard and Nat Adderley on trumpet, Cannonball Adderley, Jackie McLean, Lou Donaldson, Gigi Gryce and Phil Woods on alto, Sonny Rollins, Jimmy Heath, Benny Golson, Oliver Nelson, Stanley Turrentine, Joe Henderson, Wayne Shorter and Yusef Lateef on tenor, Pepper Adams, Cecil Payne and Nick Brignola on baritone, J. J. Johnson, Curtis Fuller, Jimmy Knepper, Frank Rehak and - more recently - Steve Turre (b.1948) on trombone, Tommy Flanagan, Cedar Walton, Bobby Timmons, Red Garland, Wynton Kelly, Joe Zawinul, Junior Mance and Ramsey Lewis on piano. Guitarists Kenny Burrell, Joe Pass and Grant Green must be included in this list, but the jazz guitarists to receive most critical acclaim were Barney Kessel (b.1923) and Wes Montgomery (1923-1968). "Montgomery developed the unorthodox technique of striking the strings with the fleshy ball of his right hand thumb, rather than the more customary practice of using a flat pick. The resulting velvet tone was further thickened by his penchant for doubling melodies and single line improvisations with another note, an octave above or below." [12]

Prominent drummers in the hard bop style included Philly Joe Jones, Louis Hayes, Art Taylor, Elvin Jones, Max Roach, Art Blakey, Roy Haynes, and Jimmy Cobb. Bass players Paul Chambers, Reggie Workman, Percy Heath, Sam Jones and Bob Cranshaw were outstanding.

Charles Mingus

"His accomplishments surpass in historic and stylistic breadth those of any other major figure in jazz," wrote author Barry Kernfeld about Charles Mingus (1922-1979).[13] It is hard to disagree with this assessment. Yet, for inexplicable reasons, Mingus's legacy seems to lack the recognition it deserves.

The bassist and composer grew up in Los Angeles. He played with Kid Ory in 1942, then toured as a bass player in the bands of Louis Armstrong and Lionel Hampton. Later, in 1950/1 in Red Norvo's Trio, with guitarist Tal Farlow, he gained national recognition. In New York, in the early 1950s, Charlie Mingus (only later in his career did he become known as Charles) worked with Billy Taylor, Charlie Parker, Stan Getz, Bud Powell and Art Tatum.

Mingus was one of the great bass players of the day, with a wide historical view of the music, combined with a tremendous technique. He played on one of the greatest bebop recordings, the Charlie Parker/Dizzy Gillespie *Quintet of the Year,* with Max Roach and Bud Powell. The year in question was 1953. He recorded the concert himself, on his own machine, at Massey Hall, in Toronto.

Listen carefully to the recording. At times you will hear two bass lines. Dissatisfied with the level of the volume of his playing on the recording, Mingus later re-recorded the bass parts.

From that time onward his compositional activities became more prominent. *The Black Saint and the Sinner Lady, Better Git It In Your Soul* and *Fables of Faubus* are some of the better known Mingus compositions. In 1977 he was diagnosed with ALS (Lou Gehrig's disease, a degeneration of the motor neurone system), and died two years later. [14]

His music lives on, less in small group and jam session recordings than in performances by larger ensembles. Groups as different as the Woody Herman Band and the Lincoln Center Jazz Orchestra have Mingus compositions in their repertoire.

Mingus's autobiography, *Beneath the Underdog,* appeared in 1971.[15]

Soul Jazz and Funk

Names change their meanings. The two words soul and funk initially described jazz that was a sub-category of hard bop. They were both hard bop simplified, with a stronger beat. The Hammond B3 electronic organ played a conspicuous role, as did gospel singing. Leading performers in this genre, which was current in the decade from 1955, were singer Ray Charles, organist Jimmy Smith, trumpeter Lee Morgan (1938-1972, whose life was cut short when he was shot dead in Slug's jazz club in New York), saxophonist Cannonball Adderley and pianists Bobby Timmons, Herbie Hancock and Horace Silver.

A word of caution is offered. The words 'soul' and 'funk' have been used again in jazz, so they are imprecise if you wish to designate a style. During the 70s they described the sort of music made popular by Aretha Franklin and James Brown.

Miles Davis

Miles Davis (1926-1991) was the son of a wealthy Illinois dentist. When he was two, the Davis family moved to St. Louis. His father bought him a trumpet for his thirteenth birthday. Miles began working in local bands during his teens. In 1944 Billy Eckstine was leading a touring big band which featured some of the foremost bop musicians, including Dizzy Gillespie, Art Blakey and Charlie Parker. The Eckstine band had a two-week engagement at the Riviera Club in Davis's home town. Billy Eckstine remembers meeting Miles Davis for the first time: "When I first heard him, he was working in St. Louis, which is Miles's home. He used to ask to sit in with the band. I'd let him so as not to hurt his feelings, because then Miles was awful. He sounded terrible; he couldn't play at all." [16]

The Birth of the Cool nonet, already discussed, was only the first of several influential Miles Davis bands. During the early 1950s Davis made many recordings with his Quintet, culminating in four albums issued by the Prestige record label in 1956. The personnel for these sessions was a front line of Davis and tenor saxophonist John Coltrane, with a rhythm section of pianist Red Garland, bassist Paul Chambers and drummer Philly Joe Jones.

These records were also characterized by Davis's use of the Harmon mute, mostly with the central stem (shank, or tube) removed, the trumpet recorded close into the microphone. The appearance of Miles Davis, with Thelonious Monk, at the 1955 Newport Jazz Festival marked the end of the trumpeter's five year struggle with heroin. The Festival was a great critical success, universally lauded as triumphant. "Miles played thrillingly and indicated that his comeback is in full stride," wrote critic Jack Tracy.[17] That autumn, Miles tied with Dizzy Gillespie for first place in the *Down Beat* critics' poll.

Miles Ahead (1957) was a Gil Evans collaboration, this time featuring Miles on flugelhorn throughout. Miles was not the first jazz musician to double on the flugelhorn, which is a trumpet-shaped valved brass instrument with a conical bore and widely flared bell. Clark Terry and Shorty Rogers had played the instrument before him, as had Chet Baker. In 1936 Joe Bishop had used the flugelhorn in Woody Herman's band. However, it was undoubtedly due to Miles's influence that the flugelhorn now became popular with players.

In 1958 the Miles Davis Quintet was augmented by the addition of Cannonball Adderley on alto saxophone. The ensuing album, *Milestones,* was a pivotal recording for Miles Davis. It was also important in the development of jazz, for it featured improvisations on modes.

Modern jazz had become more complex in terms of its harmonic foundation. Davis himself had attempted to battle with this, at one time vowing that he would 'learn all the chords.' His statement is revelatory in its naivety, akin to a painter attempting to know all the colors. His discussion of this problem with the composer George Russell (a member of what critic Eric Nisenson later called the 'Jazz Bloomsbury' that would meet in Gil Evans's apartment), led to Russell's attempt to help.

This took the form of Russell's little-understood book *The Lydian Chromatic Concept of Tonal Organization.*[18] In turn, this paved the way for Davis's modal experiments. Of course, there is more to Russell's book than the summary (see panel) would suggest. Nevertheless, what is described is at the heart of the matter. It is a simple idea, one that had already been explored by Stravinsky, Bartók and others. That many jazz writers describe it as complicated tells us more about those writers' knowledge of music theory (or rather, the lack of it) than about Russell's work. Yet the Lydian Concept was far-reaching. It caused contemporary musicians, and not only those in jazz, to be more aware of modes.

George Russell's book shows how a jazz musician can use scales as the basis on which to improvise, rather than thinking in terms of each chord that passes. Russell argues that the scale of G major makes a good fit against the chord of C major. It is a better fit, in his opinion, than the scale of C. He argues this convincingly. He divides the scale of C major into two tetrachords, pointing out that the upper tetrachord, G, A, B. C, reinforces the C triad. However, the lower tetrachord, C, D, E, F, moves towards F, having the effect of underlining the underlying C chord. Changing this tetrachord to C, D, E, *F sharp* creates a scale of G major. Thus an improviser would see (and hear) a chord of C, yet play notes selected from the scale of G. The scale of G major played from C to C is a *Lydian* scale or mode. The F sharp in the scale of G, introduced over the chord of C, is a *chromatic* addition or alteration. It is the *Lydian* fourth - or, if you prefer, the flattened fifth, discussed so much in the context of bebop. Hence the *'chromatic'* in the title *Lydian Chromatic Concept of Tonal Organization.*
Russell also reminded his readers (it is a fairly elementary point in the study of harmony) how some common chains of chords could be simplified for the improviser once it was realized that one scale would fit above several chords. This is part of the reason for the popularity of the two/five/one progression in jazz. One scale will fit above the complete progression.

Milestones is a superb album which succeeds on several levels, but it was the introduction of modes into jazz that gave writers and commentators much to discuss. Classical musicians had used modes in the

Middle Ages. Debussy had explored the use of modes in some of his works written at the turn of the century.[19] Yet they were new to jazz. It is informative of the state of jazz commentary that so much critical ink was spent on explanation and conjecture concerning modes, but never the simple observation that on the *Milestones* track *the rhythm section slows down*! Perhaps that is why Cannonball quotes Gershwin's *Fascinating Rhythm* at the opening of his solo? He had noticed.

Simplicity was also one of the cardinal aims of *Porgy and Bess* (1958), with a big band arranged by Gil Evans. Gershwin's tunes give little scope for a modal approach, but during the improvisations there are passages where a single scale is used, or a single chord.

Modality returned to the fore in 1959 in the sextet's recording of *Kind of Blue,* with the much lauded track *So What,* which has become a jam session standard. The piano voicing used in the 'amen' response figure has been accorded the status of having its own name. Called, naturally, the 'So What chord', it is a rootless voicing, comprised of a stack of fourths with a third on top.

Miles Davis went on to add to his importance in jazz history, as discussed in chapter eight. Bill Evans was the pianist on the majority of the tracks of *Kind of Blue.* The tenor saxophonist was John Coltrane. Both men were deeply influential, subsequently widely imitated and emulated.

Bill Evans

Bill Evans (1929-1980) was born in New Jersey. He began piano at the age of six, taking up the violin a year later. He won medals for playing Mozart and Schubert. By the time he entered his teens he had changed to flute as his second instrument, and was depping for his brother on piano in local dance bands. For four years, from the age of seventeen, his formal study in music education and piano continued at Southeastern Louisiana College in New Orleans. After military service, Evans's first professional work was with guitarist Mundell Lowe, when the pianist settled back in the New York area. Significantly, Evans met George Russell in 1955, and there were several projects where they co-operated. Russell's *Lydian Chromatic Concept* had been first published in 1953. Russell's ideas influenced Evans.

Bill Evans made an album for Riverside in 1956. He worked with Charles Mingus, before he replaced Red Garland in the band of Miles Davis in 1958. With John Coltrane (tenor), Cannonball Adderley (alto), Paul Chambers (bass), Jimmy Cobb (drums) and Miles on trumpet, he recorded *Kind Of Blue*. Other recordings with Miles Davis include *1958 Miles, Miles Davis and Thelonious Monk at Newport* and *Jazz at the Plaza*. Evans left Davis to form a trio with the brilliant bassist Scott LaFaro (1936-1961) and drummer Paul Motian. After LaFaro's tragic death in a car accident, Evans hired bass players Chuck Israels and Gary Peacock. Later there was a second, equally influential, trio with bassist Eddie Gomez.

Mention must also be made of *The Blues and the Abstract Truth,* with Oliver Nelson (1961), *Portrait of Cannonball* with the Cannonball Adderley Quintet, and two albums with singer Tony Bennett. An introverted, gentle player, Evans's lyricism influenced pianists Keith Jarrett, Chick Corea, Joe Zawinul, Herbie Hancock, and a host of lesser-known players.

John Coltrane

John Coltrane (1926-1967) had previously played in bands led by Dizzy Gillespie, Earl Bostic and Johnny Hodges. From the late fifties on, his career seems to represent a one-man evolutionary path. He explored the ultimate in 'time and changes' with *Giant Steps* (1959). Then, in the live album *Impressions,* we can hear his ability to play extremely long solos, in one instance for an uninterrupted fifteen minutes.

His evolution continued. In 1960 Coltrane recorded *The Avant-Garde* with trumpeter Don Cherry, bassist Charlie Haden and drummer Eddie Blackwell. Three of the tracks were Ornette Coleman compositions, appropriately, as this was actually the Coleman band with John Coltrane replacing Ornette.

In 1964 came the unexpected *A Love Supreme.* This had a strong religious content, hitherto rarely a feature of small group jazz. Within one year the album sold half a million copies.

A lasting and unusual result of *A Love Supreme* is the founding of the African Orthodox Church of Saint John Coltrane in San Francisco. Members of the Church of St. John perform portions of *A Love Supreme* with each service. Everyone in attendance is encouraged to bring an instrument to play, with the entire congregation breaking periodically into frenzied solo improvisations. According to information on the church's website, "On some occasions the riot of noise can seem miraculous, filling the room with an overwhelming spiritual passion. On other visits the combination of jazz virtuosos, hippies jamming and older men playing Kenny G style lite jazz just seems weird." [20]

Then, in 1965, Coltrane recorded *Ascension.* The lineup included four other saxophonists, two trumpeters and a rhythm section. This was fierce collective improvisation. To the casual listener it presented two vinyl sides of savage noise.

Coltrane had taken a critical battering for many years. The English poet and jazz critic Philip Larkin was particularly hard on him. Even at Coltrane's death he wrote of the saxophonist's 'squeaking and gibbering.' Larkin just did not get it, reminding one of British journalist Benny Green's assertion: "After Parker, you had to be something of a musician to follow the best jazz of the day." [21] With the absence of melody, harmony and rhythm in the new jazz, one wonders exactly what appreciative advantage would be conferred by being 'something of a musician'.

Within a year of *Ascension,* Coltrane was declining engagements. He died of cancer of the liver in July, 1967.

Why Was John Coltrane Important?

- John Coltrane contributed a repertory of melodic fragments and patterns that influenced generations of improvisers.

- He raised playing on chord changes to a new level of intensity, given the name 'sheets of sound'.

- He popularized the soprano saxophone. Hitherto, Sidney Bechet (who died in 1959) had been the only major jazz figure who had been associated with the instrument over a long period.

- With Miles Davis, he popularized modal improvisation.

- His saxophone tone influenced the conception of younger players.

- His interest in Indian music predates the much proclaimed exploration of the genre by the Beatles. His compositional use of drones (usually played by the double bass) is a result of the Indian influence.

- His free jazz work brought attention and credibility to other free musicians.

Coltrane had an enormous influence on the next generation of saxophonists. "Influences are dan-ger-ous things," pianist Paul Bley wisely observed. "In the jazz world, if you're in love with another jazz player who's a major player, especially if he plays the instrument that you play, there's a danger of being overwhelmed by the records of that person, making it difficult for you to find your own voice. So you have to be very careful about your passions...I think we've all had enough of Coltrane saxophonists. *There's* a case of somebody ruining a generation of saxophonists, as Louis Armstrong may have ruined a generation or two of trumpet players." [22]

Michael Brecker

Michael Brecker (b. 1949) is a superstar of contemporary jazz. The 'most recorded living jazz saxophonist' is claimed, though Brecker himself seems far too modest to make such a declaration. The assertion made on the saxophonist's website, that Brecker 'is among the most studied instrumentalists in music schools throughout the world' [23] is credible. The influence of Brecker's version of John Coltrane's middle-period playing on a generation of tenor players has been immense. His early work included gigs with Billy Cobham, Dreams, Steps Ahead, Horace Silver, James Taylor and Yoko Ono. With his brother Randy he formed the Brecker Brothers, one of the foremost fusion units. Brecker freelanced with many artists, including

John Abercrombie. Various tours in Europe and Asia - featuring material from the *Directions in Music* CD (2001), with Herbie Hancock, trumpeter Roy Hargrove, bassist John Patitucci and drummer Willie Jones - filled large concert halls worldwide. Brecker's unaccompanied eleven-minute solo on Naima was outstanding.

More About Miles

In 1963 Miles Davis hired a new rhythm section, comprising pianist Herbie Hancock (b.1940), double bassist Ron Carter (b.1937), and drummer Tony Williams (1945-1997), who was only seventeen years old when he joined. Their February 1964 live album *My Funny Valentine,* made in the Philharmonic Hall, New York, is one of the highest points in his interpretation of jazz standards.

Here Miles launched the idea of the rhythm section changing tempi and rhythms beneath the soloist. No longer did the music charge along relentlessly with a quarter note bass line and hi-hat on two and four. Variety took over. The idea of double time passages had been used in jazz long before this, but the *My Funny Valentine* recording introduced something far more thoughtful, far more subtle, far better integrated into the whole performance.

During the Philharmonic Hall concert Davis employs two different kinds of sound signals (probably with visual signals as well) to cue the rhythm section. One signal is a short diatonic phrase of quarter notes or eighth notes, played in half time for one or two bars. The other signal is short chromatic phrases in irregular triplet groups. These signals are typically used to change a basic pulse into double time. In this way, the pulse and shape of the music shift constantly, but seamlessly. Hancock, Carter and Williams contribute by initiating some of the interplay. George Coleman's tenor saxophone contribution is masterly.

The whole concept works. Many commentators have praised the album, but few have written about the exact way Miles and the rhythm section achieved these changing tempi.

Most critics hailed the rhythm section as the best yet. Nobody disagreed.

Free Jazz: The First Recording

Ornette Coleman (b.1930) started the free jazz revolution. Free Jazz came to prominence in the 1960s. Coleman's early albums were *Something Else* and *Tomorrow is the Question,* issued in 1958 and 1959. The name of the genre came from Coleman's album *Free Jazz,* of 1960, a free collective improvisation played by two quartets, one on each stereo channel. Free jazz has also been called 'Free Form'. In Europe, particularly in England, it is often described as 'Improvised Music'.

The term 'free' is used because the improvisations are not connected with the harmonic structure of the theme (when a theme is used). Nor is the length of the improvisation connected with the length of the theme. Yet to assume that free jazz is free of 'rules' or conventions would be wrong. Plainly, there are rules. Were a free improviser to use the vocabulary of other, more conventional, jazz styles, or to play melodically within the discipline of a key scheme (for instance, by playing a simple tune), it would be unacceptable as authentic free jazz. Surprisingly, the landmark precursor of free jazz was a famous session in 1949 that produced *Intuition* and *Digression,* under the leadership of Lennie Tristano.

Alto saxophonist Lee Konitz was a sideman. "In our rehearsing together we spent quite a lot of time going through those intricate lines that we were playing. And once in a while we got into a nice playing situation after playing the lines and - I don't remember exactly how this

140

happened, but Tristano said 'Let's just improvise freely,' and we were all very excited about the results of that." [24]

This was not the only early example of experiments with the techniques of free jazz. In 1954, Jimmy Guiffre, with Shelly Manne and Shorty Rogers, had recorded *Abstract 1,* and *Etudiez Le Cahier* ('study the exercise book'), both collective free improvisations.

These early experiments seemed to have escaped derogatory comment. But after Ornette Coleman's first efforts, free jazz had a varied reception. Some critics were enthusiasts. Among the supporters of Ornette Coleman's early work, the composer Leonard Bernstein was a leading champion. The great academic Gunther Schuller wrote about Coleman enthusiastically. Respected historian Mark Gridley praised Coleman's composition: "Coleman is one of the freshest, most prolific post-bop composers; he has written every tune on each of more than twenty albums. His style is quite original, and he has an exceptional gift for melody...Coleman's impact has been especially notable in pianist Keith Jarrett, who has written and improvised in the style of Coleman as well as dedicating a tune to him: *Piece for Ornette.*" [25]

Others were tough. Charles Mingus was hostile, knowing that Ornette Coleman had stumbled on his 'freedom' by misunderstanding how the alto saxophone's E♭ transposition functions. The English critic Benny Green wrote about Ornette Coleman and "some nebulous lunacy called Free Form." [26] Some outstanding players shifted between free jazz circles and more conventional arenas.

At several points in the evolution of jazz there have been moves to increase the appeal of the music by making it more simple. At the height of the swing era, Eddie Condon, Pee Wee Russell and other Chicagoans were playing a delightful and enduring antidote to what Condon called 'Riffitis Monotonous', that is, what they saw as the tendency for the popular big swing bands to resort too often to the repetitive and ultimately threadbare device of the riff. Their corrective was a joyous, swinging Chicago Dixieland, the recordings of which still sound uplifting and spirited today.

Of course, in its own way, bop was a rebellion against the suits of the bands, though one cannot argue that bop was by any means a return to simplicity.

At around the same time began the back-to-the-roots movement of the Revivalists. They sought to restore jazz to the modest instrumentation and aural tradition of its New Orleans origins. The ultimate in simplicity was seen in the skiffle groups and spasm bands associated with the revival movement. Domestic utensils such as the washboard and the jug, and primitive instruments such as the kazoo and the tea chest bass, were used. This was the absolute limit in breaking jazz away from standard instruments.

Later, as a reaction to the complex chromatic harmonies that underlay much of bebop, Miles Davis, George Russell and others had explored the modal system. Again, this was to achieve simplification. The introduction of modes gave a soloist freedom to play on just seven notes, rather than having to negotiate a complex fast-moving chord progression. All of the above should be borne in mind when considering the philosophy of free jazz.

Some listeners have a keen ear for harmony. Such fortunate people perceive the connection between a melody and the music that lies beneath it. They are sensitive to the note choices of an improviser, can recognize a standard tune from its chord progression, and can appreciate the skill of an improviser as he or she weaves a new melody above the harmonic background provided by the rhythm section. For those listeners, jazz is replete with meaning.

It was easy for almost any casual listener to follow the link between chords and melodic line in the paraphrased melodic line created by, say, a Dixieland trumpet player. Usually, it is simple to hear these connections in a typical blues guitar solo, or in a swing style piano solo. But once jazz reached the complexities of bebop, with its instrumental virtuosity, chord substitutions, superimpositions, anticipations, retardations and chromatic sideslips, its logic escaped the average fan. There is little doubt that some listeners heard most modern jazz improvisation as a sort of musical scribble. Its speed and complexity could overwhelm a lay audience. We cannot know what others hear, but it can be guessed that many were listening to a superficial effect rather than to a vertical structure that they understood. In a similar way, only a small proportion of the many listeners to classical music will be able to follow the progress of sonata form.

From this appreciation of superficial impact rather than internal logic it was but a short step to the *effect* of complexity being sufficient in itself. The sound of scribble could be achieved by throwing away all constraints, and producing a music that merely resembled a wilder version of bebop, but without the underlying structure and logic. The parallels with the paintings of Jackson Pollock (1912-1956) and Mark Rothko (1903-1970), and the chance (aleatoric) experiments of John Cage (1912-1992) in contemporary music, are clear.

Free Jazz could also be regarded as another attempt at simplification though, paradoxically, the end effect was complex and could not be 'understood' (in a musical sense) by anyone - not even by the players themselves. There was no more to 'understand' (in the traditional terms of melody, harmony and rhythm) than there was anything to understand in terms of criteria such as perspective, vanishing point and composition in one of Mark Rothko's blank canvasses. What was to be understood was the emotional or psychological effect of the music. Free Jazz demanded to be judged by new critical precepts.

In many respects the arrival of free jazz was a healthy event - an edgy, challenging way forward for jazz, a way past the ever more dead hand of the big band revival movement and the nostalgia crowd on one side, and the thin gruel of some of the jazz-tinged rhythm and blues combos on the other. However, it was regarded as less healthy by those who had polished their improvising expertise alongside traditional, conventional, instrumental performance skills - those players who were proficient music readers, who could play a variety of instruments with a good tone and in tune. Such players - and there had been many in jazz, from the Dorsey Brothers, Artie Shaw and Benny Goodman through to Stan Getz, Phil Woods, and most of the players in Los Angeles associated with the West Coast school of jazz - could, if they wished, combine their jazz careers with work in the lucrative world of recording studios, playing for radio and television or the film industry.

Henceforward that would be more difficult to achieve, eventually becoming impossible. Unlike their 1930s predecessors, few players on today's commercial recording sessions are simultaneously pursuing a career as groundbreaking jazz artists.

The early free jazz experiments of Ornette Coleman and his colleagues now sound disarmingly genteel compared with later performances by other musicians. Coleman plays violin and trumpet, but mainly alto saxophone, initially favoring an eye-catching British Grafton saxophone made in white acrylic plastic, a similar instrument to the one that Charlie Parker had played earlier in the decade. Coleman's first essay into free jazz was *Something Else,* which appeared in 1959.

Soon the intensity of free jazz performances soared, first with the work of the brilliant and short-lived Eric Dolphy (1928-1964), who played alto saxophone, flute and bass clarinet, and his trumpeter compeer who had an even shorter life, Booker Little (1938-1961), dying of uremia (kidney failure) at the age of 23.

Esperanto and Free Jazz

In 1962 the record label ESP-Disk was founded, the creation of New York lawyer and businessman Bernard Stollman. ESP was important because, until its collapse in 1974, Stollman's label recorded many prominent avant-garde players. Stollman was an enthusiast for the international language Esperanto, hence the ESP of his new label. The label's first record had been a sing-along in Esperanto! Stollman also wrote the notes for Albert Ayler's *Spiritual Unity,* ESP-Disk's second record, in English and Esperanto. To couple a recording of free jazz, in mono, with a sleeve note in Esperanto, and to see it become an important historical album, has an irony reminiscent of the plot of Mel Brooks's musical *Springtime for Hitler* (from the 1968 film *The Producers*), in which a deliberately organized sure-fire flop becomes a success.

Ayler (1936-1970) had a brief but vivid life, laden with controversy. Described by one historian as having "one of the most original post-Ornette Coleman saxophone styles," [27] and by another as "jazz's last great individual voice," [28] Ayler's short recording career shows him to have been wild and intense at first, the epitome of new wave extremism. His playing gradually mellowed. Ayler was yet another of those jazz players who lived a tragically short life, suffering a mysterious death. His body was retrieved from New York's East River. He had been missing for twenty days, probably a suicide victim.

Important early free players included drummer Rashied Ali (b.1935), pianist Paul Bley (b.1932), drummer Milford Graves (b. 1941), bassist David Izenzon (b.1932), trombonist Roswell Rudd (b.1935), and saxophonists Pharoah Sanders (b.1940), Archie Shepp (b.1937) and John Tchicai (b.1936). In October 1964 a series of six poorly attended but ultimately influential free jazz concerts was organized in an Off-Broadway venue by trumpeter Bill Dixon. This event led to the establishment of the Jazz Composer's Orchestra, led by Michael Mantler (b.1943) and composer Carla Bley (b.1938).

John Coltrane's *Ascension* (1965) has already been mentioned. Pianist Cecil Taylor (b.1929), now as famous as Ornette Coleman, is without doubt more controversial. Some have dismissed his music as 'not jazz', but it is so replete with Taylor's own dialect of the jazz language that it seems willful to call it anything else but jazz. Other prominent free performers include the Art Ensemble of Chicago, Lester Bowie (1941-1999), Don Cherry (1936-1995) (notable both for his association with Ornette Coleman and his use of the rarely seen pocket cornet), and the saxophonist Steve Lacy (b.1934), whose composition *The Wire* gave its name to a music magazine.

Other leaders of the free movement were Sun Ra (Herman Blount, 1914-1993) and the Solar Arkestra, the British musicians Derek Bailey (guitar), Howard Riley (piano), saxophonist Evan Parker (who names Paul Desmond as one of his favorite saxophonists), Dutch percussionist Han Bennink (b.1942), German saxophonist Peter Brötzmann (b.1941), Dutch reed player Willem Breuker (b.1944), and pianist Misha Mengelberg, born in Kiev in 1935 of Dutch/German parents. Inexplicably, the free jazz movement seems to have been stronger and more durable in Europe than in America. Free jazz is particularly strong in Holland and Germany, and to a lesser extent in Britain. The reason is unclear. It is one of an increasing number of characteristics contributing to a globalization of jazz, a phenomenon to be discussed later.

One of the more endearing ensembles prominent at this time was that of Sun Ra (Herman Sonny Blount, born 1914, though various dates are claimed between 1910 and 1916), who always professed that he was Sun Ra, and came from Saturn. The latter assertion is probably untrue.

In his earlier years he was rumored to have written arrangements for the Fletcher Henderson orchestra. The Arkestra was born in the mid-fifties, an ensemble of indeterminate size, from eight players upwards, though saxophonists Pat Patrick (b.1929) and John Gilmore (1931-1995) (said to have influenced John Coltrane) always seemed to be present. The band, based in New York, participated in the so-called October Revolution organized in 1964 by Bill Dixon, and two volumes of *The Heliocentric Worlds of Sun Ra* (1965) were issued on the ESP label.

The Arkestra was unusual in several ways, one being that their repertoire ranged from swing to the outer reaches of freedom. Another was the importance given to the visual. Painted faces and colorful costumes were the norm, along with home-produced art work on album covers, the integration of groups of dancers and singers into their stage performances, and a general air of eccentricity. Sun Ra was one of the first jazz musicians to use and record with an electric piano and the Mini-Moog synthesizer. Other influential musicians to have worked with the Arkestra include violinist Billy Bang (b.1947), saxophonist Marshall Allen (b.1924), trombonist Julian Priester (b.1935), and drummer Clifford Jarvis (b.1941).

In 1965, the same year as the issue of *The Heliocentric Worlds of Sun Ra* in New York, in Chicago the Association for the Advancement of Creative Musicians (AACM) was formed by pianist Muhal Richard Abrams (b.1930). AACM was devoted to the advancement of black avant-garde jazz. An urban collective, it grew out of a group led by saxophonist Roscoe Mitchell (b.1940), featuring Lester Bowie, Malachi Favors and Joseph Jarman. The band soon became known as the Art Ensemble of Chicago, gradually finding an audience and increasing in size. Players who have been associated with the Art Ensemble of Chicago include reed player Anthony Braxton (b.1945), violinist Leroy Jenkins and trumpeter Leo Smith. Like the Arkestra, they too went in for painted faces, colorful clothing and hats (or not so colorful in the case of

Lester Bowie's trademark white laboratory coat). They combined theatricality, great integrity, intensity, and an ever-present relish of the outrageous.

Free jazz is the least popular style in jazz history. The records achieve poor sales, it receives little radio exposure, and there is evidence that - perversely - some of the protagonists and enthusiasts take a delight in challenging their listeners and emptying the halls in which they play. "Music to be endured rather than music that truly endured," wrote critic Eric Nisenson. [29]

But not all critics condemned free jazz. Cynics remembered that the older critics had been made to appear foolish when Charlie Parker's bebop records first appeared in the mid-1940s, when a *Down Beat* review gave Bird no stars. They were wary of being caught again over the first free jazz records. Few were as unequivocal as Benny Green ('nebulous lunacy') and Don DeMichael had been. Certainly they needed to forge a new set of critical yardsticks for a music that was no longer concerned with time and changes.

Asked in 2001 whether people were still outraged by free music, free saxophonist Evan Parker said, "Not the ones who come and hear it. Maybe the ones who stay away are outraged by the idea that it's still going on. But that's all right." [30]

One way in which free jazz will endure is as a color or texture, framed, its effect heightened, alongside a more conventional language. Such a device can be heard, famously, in the brilliant version of *New York, New York*, by the JazzPar prize winner Django Bates (b. 1960), from England. About this, the British *Guardian* newspaper said: "It's little wonder that Django Bates's arrangement of *New York, New York* lurched, in the composer's words, from "distinction to extinction" at its first performance during a conference for the grandees of Polygram in New York.

The piece is a riotous collection of dissonant harmonizations, impenetrably dense textures, and snatches of the US national anthem, which surface, flail about, and then drown in Bates's all-consuming sonic maelstrom." [31]

Django Bates's integration of freedom into *New York, New York* was one answer to the challenge of progressing from the extremes of free jazz without backtracking or crossing into rock.

From the late 1960s onwards there developed a loft scene in New York, where young musicians could rehearse and hone their skills, away from the established and inhibiting clubs. These lofts were in old industrial warehouses in New York City's Greenwich Village and Lower East Side. The jazz clubs of the period, such as Birdland, the Five Spot Café and the Village Vanguard, were mostly booking established conventional players and allowing minimal opportunity for free or 'out' players.

At this time many musicians participated in the loft sessions, including Lester Bowie, saxophonist Julius Hemphill (1940-1995), saxophonist Arthur Blythe (b.1940), guitarist and trumpeter Olu Dara (b.1941), flutist James Newton (b.1953), reed player Oliver Lake (b.1942) and drummers James 'Sunny' Murray (b.1937) and Rashied Ali (b.1935). The most notable was saxophonist Sam Rivers (b.1923) who set up RivBea Studio inside his SoHo loft. Other lofts were the Studio We and the Ladies' Fort. Today the lofts are a jazz phenomenon of the past. Currently, New York's free musicians can be heard at the Internet Café, Homefront, and the Knitting Factory, though the club scene is constantly changing.

Yet the loft activity was not restricted to free music. Randy Brecker observed, "In the beginning it was primarily free jazz, under the influence of [Chick] Corea, [bassist] Dave Holland, and [drummer] Barry Altschul. As for me, I'd come there to play every style of music without any preconceived ideas.

"This was in the late 1960s. "I was twenty-one years old then," remembered Brecker. "In Manhattan the loft scene was very active, concentrated in three specific buildings. I had my own loft with musicians like Dave Holland, John Abercrombie, Ralph Towner, Stanley Clarke and Lenny White. In the bass player Gene Perla's loft, guys from Boston gathered, such as [drummer] Don Alias and [composer, keyboard player] Jan Hammer. Chick Corea lived on the same floor as my brother Mike. It was always one constant jam session in these three buildings."[32]

References

1. Rattenbury, K., *Duke Ellington: Jazz Composer* (Yale University, 1990), p. 2.
2. Shapiro, N. and Hentoff, N., op. cit., pp. 225, 226, 228.
3. Ibid., pp. 232, 233.
4. Dance, S., Liner notes for The Great Paris Concert, 1989.
5. Domek, R., *Formula Tuttis and Sectional Writing in Later Ellington Works,* IAJE Research Proceedings Yearbook, Vol. xxxi, 2001, p. 122.
6. Shapiro, N. and Hentoff, N., op. cit., p. 225.
7. Tucker, M., *The Duke Ellington Reader* (New York: OUP, 1993), p. 303. Mimi Clar, 'The Style of Duke Ellington,' *The Jazz Review,* 2/3 April, 1959.
8. Goffin, R., *Jazz, From Congo to Swing* (London: Musicians Press, 1946), p. 263.
9. Schuller, G., 'Third Stream',*The New Grove Dictionary of Jazz,* ed. Kernfeld (London: Macmillan, 1991), p. 1199.
10. Ibid.
11. Adams, S., *Jazz, A Crash Course* (London: Simon and Schuster, 1999), p. 74.

12.   Ingram, A., *A Concise History of the Electric Guitar* (Pacific, MO: Mel Bay Publications, 2001), p.57.

13.   Kernfeld, B., *The New Grove Dictionary of Jazz,* op. cit., p. 778.

14.   Spencer, F. J., op. cit., p. 3.

15.   Mingus, C., *Beneath the Underdog: His world as composed by Mingus*, ed. Nel King (New York: Random House, 1971).

16.   Shapiro, N. and Hentoff, N., op. cit., pp. 369, 370.

17.   Carner, G., ed., *The Miles Davis Companion: Four Decades of Commentary* (New York: Schirmer Books, 1996), p. 59.

18.   Russell, G., *The Lydian Chromatic Concept of Tonal Organization* (Brookline, MA: Concept Publishing, 1953).

19.   Howat, R., *Debussy in Proportion: A Musical Analysis* (Cambridge University Press, 1983).

20.   http://bayarea.citysearch.com/profile?id=904844)

21.   Green, B., *Such Sweet Thunder. Benny Green on Jazz* (London: Scribner, 2001), p. 371.

22.   Stokes, W. Royal, op. cit., pp. 151, 152.

23.   http://www.imnworld.com/brecker.html

24.   Hamilton, A., op.cit., pp. 13, 14.

25.   Gridley, M.C., *Jazz Styles, History and Analysis* (New Jersey: Prentice-Hall, 1985), p. 229.

26.   Green, B., op.cit., p. 374.

27.   Gridley, M., op.cit., p. 234.

28.   Williams, R., *The Guardian,* May 25, 2001.

29.   Nisenson, E., op.cit., p. 187.

30.   *Jazz Review,* issue 18, March 2001, p. 23.

31.   *The Guardian,* March 2, 2000.

32.   Bergerot, F. and Merlin, A., *The Story of Jazz* (London: Thames and Hudson, 1991), p.133, quotation from *Jazz Hot,* Sept-Oct, 1982.

8. Fillmore, 1970

We are at the Fillmore Auditorium in 1970, in the city and port of San Francisco, Northern California. President Richard Nixon is in the White House. Travelers can now cross the Atlantic by 747 Jumbo Jet, or Concorde if they can afford it. Both in Europe and America, in people's homes color television is fast replacing black and white.

San Francisco is changing. The Haight-Ashbury district is already unsafe, a market place for drugs. The cultural and financial center of the western United States, San Francisco is one of the USA's most cosmopolitan cities. Almost one in every two San Franciscans is 'non white' - black, East Asian, Filipino, Samoan or American Indian. Many immigrants are from Spanish America, a mix that contributes a vitality to the city, particularly strongly felt in the ethnic enclaves: in Chinatown, the Italian population of North Beach, Japan Town, the Russian colony along Clement Street, the Spanish-speaking Mission community and the black culture of the Fillmore district.

The beautiful city, with its steep streets, the great vista across the bay, its quaint cable cars and views of the Golden Gate Bridge, is a haven for artists. During the 1950s the beat poets gathered here, including Allen Ginsberg and Jack Kerouac. Haight-Ashbury district was where the flower children emerged in 1967. Here also is Alcatraz Island in the Bay, the location of the notorious prison, with its memories of inmates who, in the 1930s, included Al Capone.

The Fillmore, in previous times a dance hall or a roller rink, is now the top rock venue in the world. San Francisco has become the capital of rock music. Local performers Jefferson Airplane, Janis Joplin and the Grateful Dead, are internationally known.

Look around at the fashions. Men wear flared trousers, bold flower pattern shirts, even beads. They have their hair long, onto their shoulders. Girls wear short dresses, and sometimes shorts rather than dresses, called 'hot pants'.

Rock Around the Clock was written in 1953. With the music of Bill Haley, Little Richard and Elvis Presley, rock 'n' roll burst onto the popular music scene. At first simple and energetic, but with a surprisingly jazzy feel in its 1950s versions, rock music used only small combos. They were sufficient to support the almost obligatory singer, with maybe a saxophone or a guitar added to give color. Early bands used amplification, but at very modest levels. Youngsters now largely preferred rock to dance to, and jazz record sales declined. Dance halls struggled in the change from bands of blowing musicians playing the old music to guitar and vocal combos covering the top forty. Instrumental recordings still became hits, but as rock got older, vocals were increasingly predominant. Songs were written about the change. One noted: "They've changed our local palais into a bowling alley, fings ain't wot they used t' be." [1]

That is exactly what happened, and not just in San Francisco. The large ballrooms *(palais de danse)* were empty. In the process, much jazz sounded like the music of yesteryear. For jazz, a music that had always been a byword for being aware, hip, cool and thoughtful, this was a low point.

The guitar increased in popularity. Other electric instruments were introduced, particularly the bass guitar (Fender bass) and the electric piano. Popular music became ever louder. The quarter note bass line that had underpinned everything during the first half of the century was dropped. Now an even eighth note feel predominated. Four-in-a-bar swing was no longer favored. Couples danced separately, with no contact. For the most part it was moving rather than dancing. The loudness of the music meant that they could not speak to each other. Inevitably, jazz would have to reflect these changes.

More About Miles Davis

The Hancock/Carter/Williams rhythm section had experimented with mixing the musical devices of rock with those of jazz. Electric instruments appeared in *Miles in the Sky* of 1968. In the following year *In a Silent Way* and *Bitches Brew* were issued. With them, Davis again pointed the way forward for jazz, as he had already done twice before. In his autobiography he tells of the records he was enjoying at the time: "The music I was really listening to in 1968 was James Brown, the great guitar player Jimi Hendrix, and a new group...Sly and the Family Stone."[2]

Bitches Brew (August, 1969) was an extraordinary recording. A double album, it was fiercely contemporary, combining fashionable psychedelic artwork with lowercase sleeve notes. The instrumentation and performance style were heavily influenced by rock. One of the best-selling albums in jazz, it set the pattern for the remainder of Miles's career. Further rock-influenced albums followed during the seventies. Miles's mixing of jazz and rock was not the first. Larry Coryell, Charles Lloyd, Frank Zappa (1940-1993), Jimi Hendrix and Lou Reed had all moved towards this since the mid-sixties.

From the beginning, popular music had provided the raw material for much jazz. If they did not play their own compositions, jazz musicians improvised on the best Broadway tunes and popular songs by the great tunesmiths of a golden age: Harold Arlen *(Between the Devil and the Deep Blue Sea)*, Irving Berlin *(Alexander's Ragtime Band)*, Hoagy Carmichael *(Stardust)*, Noel Coward *(Mad About the Boy)*, Vernon Duke *(Autumn in New York)*, Jerome Kern *(All the Things You Are)*, George Gershwin *(I Got Rhythm)*, Johnny Mercer *(Goody Goody)*, Cole Porter *(Night and Day)*, Richard Rodgers *(My Funny Valentine)*,

Jule (Julius, also known as Jules) Steyne *(Just In Time)*, Vincent Youmans *(Tea for Two)* and others.

These songs were written for Broadway or Tin Pan Alley. Their composers had flourished in an age when every middle-class home had a piano. Songs were arranged and sold in an edition known as a publisher's piano copy, carefully prepared to be playable, but harmonically and rhythmically complete, to suit a standard (male) singing voice. Broadway, or more specifically, Times Square is the theater district in New York. Tin Pan Alley described both the Denmark Street area of London and 28th Street between 5th and Broadway in New York, where all the popular music publishers had offices.

As in any era, there was good and bad popular music. The bad songs tended to die an early death, not only because of the filtering effect of band arrangers who could not work well with poor material. The domestic consumer, the amateur musician, did not enjoy fumbling through trite or poorly constructed music.

At their best, the songs of this era were gems of wit and invention, with crafted lyric poetry set to simple but memorable melodies, supported by fresh chromatic harmony. This was the melody and harmony on which jazz musicians loved to improvise, which band arrangers could use as an effective vehicle on which to construct an imaginative orchestration.

One of the changes that occurred with the coming of rock 'n' roll was the rise of the guitar, the electrification of the rhythm section, and the consequent decline in interest in the domestic piano. People threw out their old pianos. Piano-smashing became an organized competitive sport. During the 1960s, sales of publisher's piano copies fell rapidly. By the 1970s, some publishers issued pop songs with a melody line and guitar grid diagrams only.

Many of the songs that appeared were composed by musicians who had only a knowledge of guitar chords. Often there was little sense of convention and logic behind the part-writing (voice-leading). One heard few of the modulatory schemes that had gone to develop chromatic harmony during the two hundred years from Bach to Bernstein. Now came a shortage of new songs that were both well-known (popular) and harmonically interesting.

A jazz improviser or a jazz orchestra arranger could do very little with the type of song sung by Jerry Lee Lewis, the Monkees, Buddy Holly or Elvis Presley. Worse, after the arrival of the Beatles, rock music had captured the young audience. In 1967 the front cover of *Down Beat* proclaimed: 'Jazz as we know it is dead.' The enthusiasts and champions of jazz had to face the fact that 'times they were a-changing'.

Many jazz musicians disliked the new, more crude, styles of song-writing. James Dapogny (b.1940), pianist and editor of *Ferdinand Jelly Roll Morton: The Collected Piano Music,* a first-of-its-kind edition, once said, "I don't play anything that was written after I was born." [3] For him, like many others, the old songs were better than the new.

Much has been written about the swinging sixties. For lovers of high quality popular music the period was far from swinging. It was a disaster. Within jazz, the man to do something about this was Miles Davis.

Miles was unorthodox. Something of his nature is revealed by Phil Woods: "Frank Rehak went to jail with Miles back in the fifties when they were very close. Frank [a trombonist] straightened out and went to work for Synanon Rehabilitation Clinic. He hadn't seen Miles for years and decided to attend that evening's concert in Houston. He went backstage and sent his card via one of the many bodyguards in attendance. The guy came back with Miles's card, on the back of which was written:

"Dear Frank, I miss you and think of you often, but I'd rather not see you." [4]

His early work with Charlie Parker, his *Birth of the Cool* innovations, together with the puissant Hancock/Carter/Williams period behind him, Miles now listened to pop music. Miles wanted the popularity of rock, from a jazz slant. He took elements of rock, to create what was later to become known as jazz-rock fusion, or more simply, fusion. Acoustic instruments were replaced by electric ones, album tracks were long, percussionists were added. He introduced a total change.

The result was *In a Silent Way,* quickly followed by *Bitches Brew.* The band on *In a Silent Way* was comprised of Joe Zawinul (b.1932) on electric keyboard and organ, Chick Corea (b.1941) also on keyboards, guitarist John McLaughlin (b.1942), drummer Tony Williams (1945-1997) and saxophonist Wayne Shorter (b.1933). For *Bitches Brew,* Tony Williams was replaced by Jack DeJohnette (b.1942). *Bitches Brew* was, in jazz terms, a best-selling album. The success vindicated Miles's revisions, heading jazz away from a chaotic demise in the cul-de-sac of free jazz. Unfortunately, it also alienated the large body of loyal enthusiasts who cherished the jazz tradition of acoustic music played largely in four-four. There was a real danger that jazz, in Dan Morgenstern's words, 'was so preoccupied with the latest that it lost sight of much of the greatest'.[5] Thus jazz was dragged into the cogs of a controversy that was to continue beyond Miles's death in 1991. The contention, stoked, stirred and stimulated by Wynton Marsalis, Stanley Crouch and others, would last well into the new century.

In the early 1970s, when saxophonist Dave Liebman (b.1946) was in Miles's band, Miles plugged in to every piece of electronic gadgetry he could find. He withdrew from the scene for most of the rest of the decade, re-emerging in the 1980s as a celebrity, one that did not play trumpet much, leaving solo work largely to others - John Scofield, then

Robben Ford on guitars, Bob Berg (1951-2002) on saxophone. Now Miles enraged the traditionalists by covering pop material. Style was crucial. "This is the period in Miles' career when red and black became staple colors, leather was like a second skin and every outfit resembled a cross between Starlight Express and Quentin Crisp." [6]

Miles, never one to waste words, had a powerful onstage personality. "There was a lot of psychological stuff, good and bad," recalled Dave Liebman, who worked with Davis for two years. "He has great perception, and can read you immediately, checking your weak and strong points. His ability to control the band by a gesture, musical or non-musical, is astounding. On the gig, everywhere. He would just look at you or cue you out. That is one of the great aspects of him which is a discussion in itself: how he leads a band. One thing that he is so powerful at is bringing you out. That's why he always had the greatest guys, because he let them be great. But of course, he's constantly checking it out." [7]

His offstage personality was another matter entirely. Miles could be complex, selfish, and horribly vicious. Saxophonist Dave Liebman witnessed Davis at his worst: "Well, usually it was drugs - again, he readily admits that. I think really if there's any cause for this it's because he was basically a drug person in one way or another. A lot of the time he had some sort of drugs or pills. Not one particular kind but just an addiction to them in general. That made him lose perspective and be a maniac. Sometimes he would think somebody was coming at him with a gun. I remember one scene in Paris with a woman who traveled with us almost all the time I was with him. All I know is that I hear this amazing yelling going on. I went in the next room down the hall. He was standing over this woman with a bottle of champagne - Moët, Dom Perignon - like a $90 bottle of champagne, pouring it on her. She was on the floor and she was bruised. She said, "Miles, don't do it." It's terrible. And I go, "Miles, what are you doing, man? Stop that!" He looked at me and said, "None of your business. Get out of here." The next day she was battered; they put her in another room for a couple of days to cool out. That was the most extreme case I experienced, but he was pretty weird with women. He was not cool. It looked like he didn't like them." [8]

Why Was Miles Davis Important?

- Miles created an influential style of jazz trumpet playing.

- He popularized the use of the flugelhorn and the Harmon mute.

- Miles Davis wrote several compositions that have become jam session standards, including *So What, Milestones, All Blues,* etc.

- He was one of the first jazz musicians to move away from improvising on chords.

- Several 'turning point' recording sessions were organized by Miles.

- He employed, and gave exposure to, many jazz innovators at a crucial point in the development of their careers.

Miles Davis Sidemen

One of the legacies of Miles Davis's work was the number of jazz-rock bands that contained his former sidemen. Tony Williams's Lifetime was one of the first, with guitarist John McLaughlin and bassist Jack Bruce. Then came McLaughlin's Mahavishnu Orchestra, with Billy Cobham, drums, Jan Hammer, piano, and violinist Jean-Luc Ponty.

Chick Corea's Return to Forever brought together Lenny White, drums, Stanley Clarke, bass, and Al DiMeola, guitar. But the most enduring was the cooperation between Joe Zawinul and saxophonist Wayne Shorter, Weather Report.

To be a member of a Miles Davis band for any length of time was to be assured of a place in jazz history. Those who qualified also included Bob Berg, Ron Carter, Billy Cobham, George Coleman, Bill Evans (saxophonist), Herbie Hancock, Dave Holland, Keith Jarrett, Jack DeJohnette, Elvin Jones, Dave Liebman, Branford Marsalis, John McLaughlin, Airto Moreira, John Scofield, Wayne Shorter and Tony Williams.

Herbie Hancock

Born in Chicago in 1940, Herbie Hancock performed a Mozart piano concerto at the age of eleven with the Chicago Symphony Orchestra. His debut album with Blue Note records produced the hit *Watermelon Man,* made popular by Mongo Santamaria. In 1963 he joined the Miles Davis Quintet. During his five-year stay he appeared on the albums *ESP, Nefertiti* and *Sorcerer,* Sorcerer being one of Hancock's nicknames for Davis. His tunes *Little One, Madness, Riot* and *The Sorcerer* were all recorded by the Miles Davis Quintet.

The 1973 *Headhunters* album from his own sextet embraced rock, funk and disco. It included the hit single *Chameleon.* He won an Oscar in 1987 for the soundtrack of the film *Round Midnight,* in which he acted and played. At the time of writing he has seven Grammys to his name (including two for his 1998 *Gershwin's World*), and is a director of the Thelonious Monk Institute of Jazz in Washington, DC.

Chick Corea

Chick Corea (b.1941) followed Hancock into the Miles Davis

Quintet in 1968. He had already considerable experience as pianist in the bands of Stan Getz, Blue Mitchell and Herbie Mann (1930-2003). His playing is influenced by Bud Powell, Bill Evans and Horace Silver. He in turn influenced many of the prominent pianists of the 1970s. Like most keyboard players of this era, he played both acoustic and electric pianos.

His practice of voicing chords in fourths (which probably came from Horace Silver) was particularly effective on electric piano. His compositions *Crystal Silence, Windows, Spain, Litha* and *La Fiesta* are still popular with jazz musicians. After frequently performing Mozart's D minor *Piano Concerto,* Chick Corea wrote his own *Concerto No. One* for piano and orchestra, which he recorded with the London Philharmonic Orchestra in the 1990s.

Keith Jarrett

During the 1980s, I attended a solo piano concert by Keith Jarrett. The concert was well under way when Jarrett, standing at the keyboard - as was his habit - suddenly stopped in mid-improvisation. He pointed up to the balcony, calling out, "You! Get out! Leave!"

There was a paralyzed, minatory silence. We all looked to see where Jarrett was pointing. He was focusing on a photographer, who stood at the balcony end overlooking the stage. The photographer protested. He was an enthusiast. He was not using flash. He was not making any noise, or moving about.

All these appeals were ignored. Keith Jarrett did not play another note until an attendant arrived to escort the wrongdoer out of the hall. Jarrett perused the front rows of the audience. "Now, how do I get back into that?"

"Have a drag and try again," offered a listener.

"That may be your solution, but it isn't mine," retorted the pianist, going into an anti-stimulants diatribe.

That evening we learned a lot about the intensity of Keith Jarrett.

Jarrett (b.1945) came to prominence in the Charles Lloyd Quartet between 1966-69. After working for Miles Davis in 1971, he made his first solo album for ECM. The next year he began his solo concerts. He is best known for his solo piano albums on ECM, particularly *The Köln Concert* of 1975. He has also recorded works from the classical repertory, including Samuel Barber's *Concerto for Piano* and J. S. Bach's *Goldberg Variations* and *48 Preludes and Fugues*. Of the prominent jazz pianists of this period, only Keith Jarrett and McCoy Tyner remained loyal to the traditional acoustic piano.

Joe Zawinul

Austrian born Joe Zawinul (b.1932) emigrated to America in 1959. His first major impact on the American jazz scene was as a member of saxophonist Cannonball Adderley's band. Between 1961 and 1970 he wrote two of the band's hits, *Mercy, Mercy* and *Walk Tall*. Then Miles Davis propelled his career forward, with the use of Zawinul's *In A Silent Way* as the title track of the album. This pioneered the fusion of jazz improvisation with rock instruments and rock performance techniques. Joe Zawinul's *Pharaoh's Dance* was included in Miles Davis's *Bitches Brew* album.

Weather Report, formed in 1971, included saxophonist Wayne Shorter and bassist Miroslav Vitous. The band's 1977 album *Heavy Weather* sold more than 400,000 copies. It incorporated *Birdland*, written by Zawinul, inspired by a performance of the Count Basie band at the New York club named after Charlie 'Bird' Parker.

Zawinul is a productive jazz composer, a pioneer of the use of synthesizers and electric pianos, tone-coloring devices such as the ring modulator, and the introduction of the unusual timbres provided by the thumb piano (kalimba), tambura (an Indian classical string instrument, usually flat-backed with four strings), ocarina, steel drums, xylophone - even the unamplified piano, used as a novelty texture!

There are many other Davis sidemen from the later years who went on to successful solo careers: saxophonists Bob Berg and Kenny Garrett, guitarists Robben Ford, Mike Stern and Rick Margitza. A rich heritage of Miles is available on record, around twenty CDs from the mid-80s, for a start. Bewildering, but good to have the choice.

References

1. *Fings Ain't Wot They Used T'Be*. Song, 1959, by Lionel Bart (1930 - 1999).
2. Davis, M., with Troupe, Q., *Miles: The Autobiography* (London: Picador, 1990), p. 282.
3. Dapogny, J., broadcast interview with Marian McPartland on website: http://www.jazzbymail.com/artists/davern.html
4. Fisher, L., *Miles Davis* and *Dave Liebman: Jazz Connections* (Lampeter, Dyfed: Edwin Mellen Press, 1996), p. 11.
5. Morgenstern, D., Essay on website, *All About Jazz,* at: http://www.allaboutjazz.com/journalists/morgenstern6.htm
6. Finlay, R., *Jazz Review,* September 2002, p. 32.
7. Fisher, L., op. cit., p. 18.
8. Ibid., p. 164.

9. The Montreux Festival

Montreux is probably the most successful, most respected of European jazz festivals. The small Swiss town has a beautiful location on the shore of Lake Léman, which separates France and Switzerland at the foot of the Alps. The Festival takes place in July. We can float in a paddle boat on the lake, wander in the hills, hang out in the town, go shopping, visit the casino, drive, ride on a steam train, or sit watching our fellow festival attenders in the Montreux Jazz Café. Between these distractions, in the Miles Davis Hall or the Stravinski Auditorium, or often in the open air if the weather is kind, there are workshops to attend, and the best of jazz to be heard.

The Festival was founded by Claude Nobs in 1967, and directed by him for the rest of the century and beyond. One great strength is the long association between Claude Nobs and Atlantic Records, through Ahmet Artegun, the founder of the company. Every important Atlantic artist has appeared at Montreux. The Festival has an unusually broad-minded approach. Rock, Multi-Media, World Music, all come to the party. Artists that have appeared include pianist Lynne Arriale, blues guitarist B. B. King, Tony Bennett, Dave Brubeck, Miles Davis, George Duke, Dorothy Donnegan, Don Ellis, Bill Evans, Ella Fitzgerald, Aretha Franklin, Charles Lloyd, Charlie Mingus and the Modern Jazz Quartet. Claude Nobs ('Funky Claude') admits that some critics have said that this breadth is an insult to the word jazz.

About this he is unapologetic, claiming that the musical policy at Montreux is its great virtue. Claude Nobs has always taken an interest in the best of blues, gospel, soul and rock. In the long term this has ensured the vigor and strength of his festival, and secured its success. Today there are hundreds of large jazz festivals in Europe.

Some, such as Antibes, Vienne, Marciac, or the North Sea Festival, are world famous. In France alone there are said to be 250 festivals a year. Coming here gives attenders an opportunity to catch up with what is happening internationally.

The first three-day festival in 1967 offered saxophonist Charles Lloyd's Quartet with pianist Keith Jarrett. Trumpet player Dusko Goykovich was winner of a competition for European jazz groups. The next year, alongside pianist Bill Evans and singer Nina Simone (1933-2003), new European saxophonists John Surman and Jan Garbarek appeared. In 1970, Japanese saxophonist Sadao Watanabe played alongside arranger, composer and saxophonist Gerry Mulligan. More than 300 musicians played in the 1971 Montreux Festival, including vibraphonist Gary Burton, saxophonist King Curtis (who was murdered two months later), and singer Roberta Flack. By 1974 African music had been represented at the Festival by pianist Randy Weston, and Brazilian music by percussionist Airto Moreira and singer/composer Milton Nascimento. The Rolling Stones appeared in 1976.

By the end of the seventies the Festival had also encompassed free jazz, reggae and country music. At the beginning of the twenty-first century, over 220,000 visitors come to the Festival's main concert halls.

The Internationalization of Jazz

Since its birth, jazz has been unequivocally American. Some take exception to the description 'Afro-American music.' They argue that jazz grew from many influences. European marches, the French quadrille, East-European Jewish Klezmer, the piano styles of Franz Liszt and Frédéric Chopin, the harmonic language of Debussy, Delius, Ravel and Stravinsky, and Italian opera have all provided constituent elements to add to the richness of jazz. Yet no one suggests that jazz is Euro-American music. Cuban music and Balinese gamelan also contribute to the mix.

Therefore, as African music was only one of several influences, it is sometimes argued that it is a distortion to highlight the impact of African music over all the others by calling jazz Afro-American. Jazz has many ancestors from many places, but was born in America. Accordingly, they argue, it is correct to describe it as American music.

Several of the ensembles of jazz are unequivocally American. The big band is American. The Dixieland instrumentation of clarinet, trumpet and trombone, playing in free polyphony, is American. The piano/vibes/guitar formula of George Shearing is American. All these ensembles were devised and developed in America, nowhere else. Nevertheless, the African ingredient is clear to hear and plain to see, and the reason for the use of the Afro-American title is obvious.

Jazz continued to be an all-American music during the eras of New Orleans, Swing, Bebop, Hard Bop and Cool. Then, at a time that is difficult to pinpoint exactly, the move to internationalization began. Until the bebop era, only a few influential jazz musicians had been born outside America. The list includes gypsy guitarist Django Reinhardt, French violinist Stephane Grappelli, British bassist and arranger Spike Hughes (who first visited New York in 1933), André Hodeir (b.1921) the French critic, composer and arranger, and a few others. The move towards internationalization happened later.

After World War II, the list of important non-Americans begins to lengthen. In 1946, the British pianist (and composer of *Lullaby of Birdland*) George Shearing visited America. He settled in the States in 1947. The *Jazz at the Philharmonic* tours organized by impresario Norman Granz from 1946, increased the influence of American jazzmen overseas, though the first concert was in California. Granz had ordered a poster that read 'Jazz at the Philharmonic Auditorium'. Lacking space, the Los Angeles printer made it read *Jazz at the Philharmonic*. The name stuck, though frequently abbreviated to *Jazz at the Phil,* or just JATP.

Beginning with tours within the USA, Granz (1918-2001) organized groups of great jazz musicians, and staged jam sessions involving a parade of soloists working with a rhythm section. Not without controversy - people tended to like or loathe the setup - Granz brought Ella Fitzgerald, Stan Getz, Coleman Hawkins, Billie Holiday, Hank Jones, Oscar Peterson, Lester Young and other legendary names (even Charlie Parker and Dizzy Gillespie) to a worldwide concert-hall audience. Granz also used these tours to pioneer live recording, issuing the results on his Clef, Mercury, Norgran, Verve and Pablo labels. Norman Granz was an art enthusiast and an admirer of Picasso, hence the 'Pablo' title. Interestingly, there is an extant Picasso lithograph from 1948, called *Verve.*

The international *Jazz at the Philharmonic* tours continued until the late 1960s, by which time there was a steady flow of important overseas jazz musicians into America. Pianist/arranger Toshiko Akiyoshi from Japan, saxophonist Gato Barbieri from Argentina, pianist and drummer (and composer of *Seven Steps to Heaven*) Victor Feldman from Britain, and arranger Mike Gibbs from Rhodesia (now Zimbabwe) all arrived in the USA. Many other non-Americans worked in the American jazz world, including pianists Ronnie Ball (b. 1927) and Dill Jones (1923-1984), and saxophonists Roy Reynolds and Joe Temperley. Bassist Dave Holland, guitarist John McLaughlin, saxophonist Chris Hunter and pianist Marian McPartland, all from Britain, and keyboard player Joe Zawinul, from Austria, settled in North America. Pianist Jan Hammer left Czechoslovakia to attend Berklee College of Music, Boston, at the age of twenty.

Later it became possible for a jazz musician to be internationally known without moving permanently to the USA. French bassist Pierre Michelot, Australian multi-instrumentalist James Morrison, French pianist Michel Petrucciani (1962-1999), Algerian pianist Martial Solal, French violinist Jean-Luc Ponty, Belgian guitarist, harmonica player and composer of *Bluesette,* Toots Thielemans, and French saxophonist Barney Wilen (1937-1996) are influential non-American jazz names that come to mind.

This list must also include pianist Tete Montoliu (1933-1997) from Spain, trumpeter and *JazzPar* prize winner Enrico Rava (b.1939) from Italy, and Niels-Henning Ørsted Pedersen (b.1946), the virtuoso double bassist from Denmark.

An opposite flow has occurred. Several distinguished American jazz musicians chose to live outside the USA. In the very early days of jazz, Sidney Bechet lived in London and Paris. Coleman Hawkins lived in Europe between 1934 and 1939. Other Americans in Europe included Benny Carter before World War II, and Don Byas just after the war, in 1946. Later, Johnny Griffin and Kenny Drew were expatriates. Clarinetist Bob Wilber opted to live in the English Cotswolds. Historic Chicago tenor player Bud Freeman (1906-1991) took up residence in London towards the end of his life.

Altoist Phil Woods, later famous for his beautiful saxophone solo on the Billy Joel single *Just the Way You Are,* had success with his European Rhythm Machine band during a period when he chose to live in Europe. American trombonist Jiggs Whigham moved to Germany. Trombonist and arranger Ed Neumeister went to Vienna. Bop tenorist Dexter Gordon (1923-1990) emigrated to Paris, starred in the film *Round Midnight,* and received the award of *Chevalier de l'Ordre des Arts et des Lettres.* Flugelhorn star Art Farmer (1928-1999) lived in

Vienna for many years, American soprano saxophone player Steve Lacy lived in Paris for three decades. Other Americans playing away have included the Art Ensemble of Chicago, trumpeters Benny Bailey and Chet Baker, saxophonists Johnny Griffin, Scott Hamilton, Gerry Mulligan and Ben Webster, guitarist Jimmy Rainey and singers Dee Dee Bridgewater, Marian Montgomery (born in Natchez, 1934-2002) and Stacey Kent.

Jazz in Japan

Though first outside America to welcome jazz wholeheartedly, Europe is not unique in its enthusiasm for the music. The Japanese nation, too, has a great appetite for jazz. In *Swing Journal,* Japan has the largest circulation jazz magazine in the world. A healthy club and concert touring circuit exists in Japan, and there are successful Blue Note clubs in the cities of Tokyo and Osaka. While writing *A Concise History of Jazz,* the author visited the Tokyo Blue Note, to hear both the Count Basie Band and the Michel Camilo Trio, each appearing for a week in twice-nightly residencies.

The large and comfortable Blue Note club is very expensive by Western standards, yet on both occasions it held a capacity audience. Tidiness, good manners and kindness are exemplary in Japan. Here in the Blue Note, devotion to the music was palpable. Audience behavior was faultless, though different from the norms of New York or London. At one point during the Basie concert the entire audience clapped along on the off-beat. A charming and enthusiastic gesture, it was entirely divergent from the cooler audience dedication usually encountered in the west.

Pianist Mal Waldron has spoken enthusiastically about the reaction to jazz in Japan. "I had this record that was very popular in Japan in 1969, *Left Alone.* It won a Gold Disc award, and that record has been selling steadily in Japan ever since. I got coverage from it, and was invited to come over there in 1970, just to see the country for two weeks, by *Swing Journal.* At that time I made two records, *Tokyo Reverie* and *Tokyo Bound,* two Japanese records. Then they set me up for tours every year after that, '71, '72, '73, '75, '76, '77, '79, like that, and I kept coming back for larger tours. For example, I did two weeks the first time, then one month and two months, and three months, practically every year, right up to the present. I'm very well known there.

"Oh, the audiences are fantastic. You feel the air comin' at you and you have to lean forward. Otherwise, if you stand up straight, you go backward! Japan has the best audiences in the world, because there most of the people know about jazz and they love jazz. About 90 per cent of the people there know about jazz - the largest percentage of any country. Well, it's because of the way they're educated. They have coffee shops all over Japan where, for the price of a cup of coffee, you can hear any record that you want to hear. You just fill out a form and tell 'em what you want to hear and they have all the records there; every coffee shop has millions of records and they play them for you. One coffee shop is called the Mingus." [1]

Ramsey Lewis has expressed similar enthusiasm and affection for audiences in Europe and Japan. "The European audience takes jazz seriously; they take the music seriously; they take the performance seriously - and the same with the Japanese audience. There's not as much participation or words of encouragement *during* a performance, but at the end of the performance, all hell breaks loose.

"I'll never forget the first time we played Japan. In America, you know, you're used to, 'Go on! Yeah, man! *Awright!*' We open with a blockbuster, hit 'em right in the middle of the nose and chops, knock the shit out of 'em! So we open like that with a high-energy piece and, man, you could hear a pin drop. But at the end of the piece it was, 'Ra- a-a-ah!' standing ovation, encores, people lined up outside the stage door with their markers and special autograph cardboard, and they say things like, 'The record you did six years ago with so-and-so, and the engineer was so-and-so,' and they name the songs and say, 'I liked the way you played on the bridge.' They're *into* the *music*! I was just totally blown away! America's just beginning to get to this point." [2]

South Africa

In 1960s South Africa, against a background of a segregated society that exceeded the worst aspects of the southern states in the USA, pianist Dollar Brand, trumpeter Hugh Masekela (b.1939) and others created Township Jazz. It was to have worldwide influence. The young pianist gained the nickname 'Dollar' because he always seemed to be carrying dollars to buy the latest jazz albums. He was exposed to Meade 'Lux' Lewis, Fats Waller, Louis Jordan and other American musicians who played on the 78 rpm records sold by seamen in the international port of Capetown.

Brand (b.1934) converted to Islam in 1968, receiving the name Abdullah Ibrahim. He and Masekela were members of an all-black sextet, the Jazz Epistles, playing township bebop, a combination of bebop and African kwela. *Kwela* is penny whistle music.

Understandably, South African sounds that achieved international recognition were quickly considered passé back home. South African music followed political events. After the 1976 student uprising in Soweto, the young generation shunned the music of their parents. They embraced what they thought were the more progressive forms of soul and disco. A visitor going to black township festivals in South Africa would hear band after band playing disco music driven by banks of keyboards, rather than *mbaqanga* township jive.

Mbaqanga is the dance music of the black townships. It emerged in the 1930s, the name taken from the word for a swiftly made steamed mealie

171

bread. Hence music to make quick 'bread'. Today, *mbaqanga* bands usually include guitars, drums, bass, vocals, and perhaps brass. Incredibly, considering such strong official pressure for segregation, a multiracial group, the Blue Notes, was formed by pianist Chris McGregor in 1963. Later the band incorporated free jazz and evolved into the Brotherhood of Breath big band. This in turn influenced the European free jazz scene.

South African jazz was given a boost by the arrival in the country of Darius Brubeck, the pianist son of Dave Brubeck. As Director of the Center for Jazz and Popular Music and Professor of Jazz Studies at the University of Natal, Durban, he joined the Music Department in 1983, starting the first Jazz Studies course offered by an African University. He was to be working in a difficult context. A Congress of South African Trade Unions report published in September 2002 stated that: "South Africa has the highest unemployment of any middle-income country. The figure of almost 30% unemployment by the official definition ignores those too discouraged to seek work."

Against such difficulties, which included funding battles, inflation around 11%, and remoteness from the jazz capitals of the world, South African jazz education thrived. An association of South African Jazz Educators was formed. The annual Standard Bank National Youth Jazz Festival has taken place in South Africa since the early 1990s.

Yesterday's News

Commenting on the trend towards internationalization in jazz, journalist Mike Zwerin said, "The concept of jazz as solely American music is 'history', as Americans use that word. Washed-up, yesterday's news. Historically, America remains the inventor. But its days of sole dominion are history. New ideas come from other places now." [3]

Saxophonist Dave Liebman has made a similar point. "It's not that

America is over, or finished, but the truth is that the birthplace of music has had its time. It had its hundred years, or whatever, and the innovators were here and are done. But for this music to exist and go on, it had to get infusions from other cultures and other peoples, and it's happening. A lot of people in America are not aware of it because they're insulated and they don't get out, but people like myself, and people who travel to a lot of countries and teach, are. There are young people who are really for the most part optimistic because they are bringing something to it. It may be a Danish folk song in a jazz style, but it's an attempt to bring what they have to the music they're learning. And I think that's a very positive thing." [4]

Promoter George Wein, the man who made the first Newport Jazz Festival happen half a century ago, also recognized this trend. He is now the producer of the JVC Festival in New York (Victor Company of Japan), thought of as the world's great marquee festival. In 2000 he flooded the festival with non-American bands and what one commentator described as 'offshore artists'. It created great audience excitement.

The Internationalization of Jazz Criticism

Some of the best writing and criticism came initially from Europe. The French-speaking Belgian, Robert Goffin (1898-1984), was an early pioneer. In *Jazz, from Congo to Swing,* he says: "It would be pretentious on my part to say that I discovered jazz, but I can claim to have been the first to have paid serious attention to it. In 1919, enchanted by the Negro jazz of Louis Mitchell, I wrote a long article in a literary review, *Le Disque Vert.*" [5]

The first books of jazz commentary were Robert Goffin's *Aux Frontières du Jazz* (1930), and Hugues Panassié's *Le Jazz Hot* (1934). Panassié was also behind the first French jazz magazine, *Jazz Hot,* which began in the late 1920s, and which he edited from 1935.

In Britain, *Melody Maker,* founded in 1926, was the first magazine in the world to devote space to jazz record reviews. The prestigious American magazine *Down Beat* began publication in 1934. It is still an excellent source of commentary at the time of writing. Other significant jazz magazines include *Jazziz* (1984) and *Jazz Times* (1970) in the USA, *Crescendo* (1961), *Jazz Journal* (1948), *Jazz Review* and *JazzWise* in Britain, *Coda* (1958) in Canada, *Jazz Podium* (1951) in Germany, *JazzNytt* (Norway), and *Swing Journal* (Japan). Today, the latter has an enormous circulation, around 125,000.

Jazz Festivals

Festivals arrived relatively late during the evolution of jazz. They have an important function, particularly an economic one, allowing listeners to hear a variety of artists, letting the old and well-known musicians create an audience for the younger players, providing a platform for the new, and offering the opportunity to blend a program from a variety of styles. Taking place all over the world, they have played a major part in the internationalization of jazz.

Around the world there are hundreds of large jazz festivals. Although some of the major events have been remarkably constant affairs - Montreux and Newport are excellent examples - others come and go, or temporarily disappear and then emerge with a new name. If you are new to jazz, a visit to a festival is an ideal way to sample a variety of the music in congenial and relaxed surroundings.

References
1. Stokes, W. Royal., op. cit., pp. 73, 74.
2. Ibid., p. 88.
3. Reference at: www.mikezwerin.com/news
4. Fisher, L., op. cit., p. 18.
5. Goffin, R., op. cit., p. 1.

10. Europe: Trondheim, Norway, 1995

It is the middle of October in 1995. We are in Trondheim, Norway's third largest city, 550 kilometers north of the capital, Oslo. We are walking through the city on a fine but cold evening, towards the Nidaros Cathedral. One of the largest Gothic buildings in Scandinavia, this is where all the kings of Norway are crowned. Norway is prosperous, the second largest oil exporting nation in the world. The Norwegians, with characteristic independence, have voted to stay out of the European Union. Of the affluent European nations only they, together with Iceland and Switzerland, choose to remain apart.

Tonight in Trondheim everyone seems to be heading in the same direction, either on foot or by bicycle. Crowds of young people, mostly of university age or a little older, stream along the road. All are quiet, well behaved, sensibly dressed against the cold evening. As they walk along, one or two of these concertgoers are listening to their personal portable stereo systems, through headphones. The music is on cassette. The digital mini-disc, though now available, has not yet achieved significant sales. Enthusiasm is in the air, a feeling of anticipation, for we are all going to hear a concert of some very unusual music.

Tonight's concert is to be given by the Norwegian saxophonist Jan Garbarek, together with a Renaissance group from Britain, the Hilliard Ensemble. A year ago these musicians recorded a CD, *Officium,* on the ECM label, in which the all-male vocal ensemble sang medieval music while Jan Garbarek played alto and tenor saxophone improvisations in and around the singing. A novel idea, as with many projects emanating from the ECM label it sold sufficiently well to be regarded as a jazz hit. Not surprisingly, the opportunity to hear this music played in such appropriate surroundings, with a Norwegian national jazz hero Jan Garbarek on home ground, has proved popular. Two performances will take place tonight. The cathedral is full for both.

To older jazz fans, this popularity is a surprise. The music does not have a rhythm section, it does not swing, you cannot dance to it, it does not have catchy tunes, Garbarek does not play groovy licks. The music is quiet, the harmonic language is archaic, and it does not have obvious climaxes. Saxophonist Garbarek is certainly improvising, but some knowledgeable listeners debate, fruitlessly, whether the music should be called jazz.

Nidaros Cathedral's geometry and acoustics are exploited by the performers. The concert opens with a quadrophonic effect, as the singers are first heard from all four corners of the building. They begin to sing out of sight of the audience. Gently, dramatically, the music builds as they come into view, walking slowly towards their meeting point at the center of the enormous space. Only then does Jan Garbarek start his improvisation, his saxophone commenting on, and paralleling, the vocal parts. Naturally we knew what we were coming to hear, but no CD can produce this glorious acoustical and dramatic effect.

A sense of occasion prevails here tonight. We are lucky to be present.

ECM

In 1969, bass player and record producer Manfred Eicher founded the record label Edition of Contemporary Music, ECM. Eicher had previously been employed by another record company, working on the production of orchestral and chamber music. He felt that the same love and care that was lavished on those recordings should be brought to the production of contemporary jazz records. Though Eicher did not express it in this way, there had long been a faint but detectable tendency among jazz supporters to pursue the illusion of European respectability. This respectability of European classical music was what was coveted; the disdain towards jazz that this has produced is no less strong in Europe than elsewhere. It is still alive today.

Rock was enjoying great popularity at the time. Eicher was concerned that many important young jazz players were being overlooked. His company's first pressings on vinyl used the highest quality materials. Each recording had to subsidize the next. Fortunately, the early releases, first with American pianist Paul Bley, then with Norwegian saxophonist Jan Garbarek, were successful. The good fortune continued, despite Eicher's pursuance of a policy that, by industry mores, was not commercial.

By 2002 the ECM company, based in Munich, had a catalog of more than 700 titles, and was celebrating the success of *Morimur,* a radical reinterpretation of Bach's *Partita in D Minor for Solo Violin,* a collaboration between the Baroque violinist Christopher Poppen and four singers - from the Hilliard Ensemble again. So, not all the titles were jazz. ECM was, and remains, almost impossible to define, but much of the company's catalog is irrefutably jazz, or jazz influenced.

In the words of the British newspaper, *The Independent,* celebrating the label's thirtieth birthday in 1999, "The ECM label and its founder Manfred Eicher have altered musical history. The company has become the most important imprint in the world for jazz and new music. After 30 years, their albums still range over the eclectic and the unclassifiable - and have a sound world as distinctive as the record sleeves' famous austere design." [1]

The visual style consists of muted colors, and a consistent, plain typeface. Moody, ascetic monochrome photography is favored, empty landscapes with enigmatic images are common. The style extends to the sound quality of the recordings, most of which Manfred Eicher still produces himself.

The austerity is as thoroughgoing and consistent as it is special. When I made my first visit to the headquarters of ECM, in a pleasant suburb to the north of the Bavarian city of Munich in Germany, I was directed to premises above a supermarket. No sign on the building identified it as the ECM offices. Access was through the supermarket checkout, by way of a door in the wall. Then I stumbled up a gloomy staircase bearing a diminutive sign saying 'ECM Records'. Once inside, the offices were smart, tasteful and businesslike. The reception and hospitality offered was kind and generous. But the lack of outward display was truly exceptional, particularly in a profession - selling records - not normally known for its reticence or modesty. This seemed consistent with the ECM image.

Landmark recordings on ECM include the early *Afric Pepperbird* (1970), by Norwegian saxophonist Jan Garbarek (b.1947), Garbarek's later pairing with the Hilliard singers, *Officium* (1993), in which saxophone improvisations are set against medieval church music, Keith Jarrett's *The Köln Concert*, released in 1975 and which sold more than two million copies, recordings by saxophonist John Surman (b.1944), issues by former Garbarek drummer Edward Vesala (b.1945) which incorporate *Ode to the Death of Jazz,* and several recordings that have little to do with jazz, including bandoneon player Dino Saluzzi (b. 1935). (The bandoneon is an Argentinian type of button accordion.)

Also in the catalogue was Turkish influenced improvised music by Anouar Brahem with clarinetist Barbaros Erköse, a fascinating series of recordings of improvised world music by Stephan Micus, and several composed-ensemble albums by Edward Vesala the Finnish drummer and composer. An artist significant to ECM, Eberhard Weber, launched the thumbprint sound of the label with *The Colors of Chloé*. Others who recorded for ECM include John Abercrombie, Gary Burton, Chick Corea, Egberto Gismonti, Dave Holland, Pat

Metheny, Terje Rypdal, Ralph Towner, Eberhard Weber, Kenny Wheeler and Norma Winstone.

Bassist Glen Moore was generous in his praise of ECM, crediting Manfred Eicher with keeping the band Oregon (Paul McCandless, reeds, flute, Glen Moore, bass, violin, piano, Ralph Towner, guitar, piano, synthesizer, Collin Walcott, sitar, percussion, voice) together. "Oregon was the real beacon through that whole thing. Oregon really stayed in existence because of Manfred Eicher at ECM. He invited us to record. ECM organized tours for us in Europe. We went from playing in these little bars where we had to clean the floor and put down the lines of baking soda to keep the cockroaches off our instruments to going to Europe and playing in the radio houses and beautiful halls and in Vienna where Beethoven conducted and where Mozart had played. ECM really gave us the opportunity to feel like adult musicians, away from America, where there'd always been a lot more pop emphasis and all this electric kind of superstar feeling. Because of ECM, we were able to hang in there." [2]

The JAZZPAR prize

Sometimes called The Jazz Oscar, or the Nobel Prize of Jazz, the world's largest international jazz award of its kind, presented every year solely to people from the jazz world, is the Danish JAZZPAR Prize. At the time of writing it carries a financial presentation equivalent to approximately $27,000, which is awarded at an annual concert in Copenhagen, the final concert in a Prize Concert Tour. The money is given to an internationally known and fully active jazz artist who is especially deserving of further acclaim. Former winners are Muhal Richard Abrams (1990), David Murray (1991), Lee Konitz (1992), Tommy Flanagan (1993), Roy Haynes (1994), Tony Coe (1995), Geri Allen (1996), Django Bates (1997), Jim Hall (1998), Martial Solal (1999), Chris Potter (2000), Marilyn Mazur (2001), Enrico Rava (2002) and Andrew Hill (2003).

References

1. *The Independent,* quoted April 1999, on ECM website http://www.ecmrecords.com/
2. Stokes, W. Royal, op. cit., p. 164.

11. Jazz at Lincoln Center, New York

The Lincoln Center is at Broadway and 64th, in Manhattan, on the West Side near to Central Park, a modern complex of concert halls, opera houses and open-air plazas. In recent years there has been an association between the Lincoln Center and jazz, as represented by the virtuoso trumpeter Wynton Marsalis. Jazz at Lincoln Center (J@LC) is one of twelve constituent organizations on the campus of Lincoln Center for the Performing Arts.

The relationship began with Wynton's *Jazz at Lincoln Center* series, for which he is cofounder and Artistic Director. The series has run since 1987, presenting recreated historical performances. The concerts have drawn capacity audiences. Showcasing some of the best young players, it includes trumpeters Nicholas Payton and Wallace Roney, and clarinetist Dr. Michael White. Now there is a fifteen-strong Lincoln Center Jazz Orchestra. Directed on stage by Marsalis, it employs players such as Victor Goines (saxophones), Marcus Printup (trumpet), Ted Nash (saxophones), Rodney Whitaker (bass) and Joe Temperley (baritone).

At the beginning of the new century, Wynton Marsalis is featured prominently as a commentator and performer in a television mini series on jazz, and fronts the Lincoln Center Jazz Orchestra on national and international tours. Not everyone agrees with Wynton's view of jazz and jazz history. Nevertheless, he has assumed the role of an articulate and enthusiastic spokesman for jazz around the world. J@LC also organizes a major youth band competition, *Essentially Ellington*. Several radio stations are devoted exclusively to jazz. Some of these can be heard anywhere in the world, via the Internet. Classic jazz films are available on DVD, though terrestrial television, which has long relegated arts programs to off-peak spots, virtually ignores jazz.

Recently a $130 million project building was completed, and Frederick P. Rose Hall is the new home of Jazz at Lincoln Center. This is the world's first performing arts facility designed specifically for jazz education, performance and broadcasting. Located at Columbus Circle, components include a 1,300 seat concert theater, a 700 seat performance space, a 140 seat jazz café, the Irene Diamond Education Center, and the Ertegun Jazz Hall of Fame, an interactive multimedia history of jazz. Maybe we will meet there?

The New Conservatives; Wynton Marsalis

Wynton Marsalis was born in New Orleans in 1961. The beginning of his professional life overlapped with the final decade of Miles Davis's career. Wynton's father, New Orleans pianist Ellis Marsalis, has four sons: saxophonist Branford, trombonist and producer Delfeayo, drummer Jason, and Wynton. Before the ascent to worldwide fame of his sons, Ellis was best known as an educator, whose students included trumpeter Terence Blanchard, saxophonist Victor Goines, saxophonist Donald Harrison, singer Harry Connick Junior and trumpeter Nicholas Payton.

By the age of fourteen Wynton, a superb trumpet player by any standards, had performed the Haydn *Trumpet Concerto* with the New Orleans Philharmonic. At the age of eighteen he began studying at the Juilliard School of Music in New York, commencing as a pit musician in *Sweeny Todd,* and on gigs with the Brooklyn Philharmonic. During a twelve-month stint with Art Blakey, he recorded before his nineteenth birthday. Soon after, he was working with the Herbie Hancock Quartet (Ron Carter, bass, Tony Williams, drums). By 1982 *Down Beat* readers had voted him Jazz Musician of the Year. His debut LP *Wynton Marsalis* was chosen as *Jazz Album of the Year,* and he was named 'Number One Trumpet'.

Most notably, he defeated Miles Davis in each category. Wynton has won eight Grammy Awards, and received the 1997 Pulitzer Prize in Music for his album on the subject of slavery, *Blood on the Fields.* He is one of the few musicians who can work convincingly at the highest levels in both jazz and classical music, able to satisfy the most exacting standards of each genre.

The first musician to be triumphantly successful in the two cultures was Benny Goodman. While near to his heyday as King of Swing, Goodman embarked on an exploration of European Concert Music. Inverted snobbery ensured that this cost him much status in the jazz world, but no objective listener can question Goodman's right to stand as the pioneer figure among that rare breed of musicians who can pass happily between jazz and straight.

A few other musicians followed. André Previn (b.1929) made some lithe and blithe small group jazz albums in the 50s before emerging as the conductor of the London Symphony Orchestra in the 1960s. After Goodman and Previn, the list of colossi that bestride the two cultures begins to tail off. This is not to belittle the several first-rate musicians who worked at the top end of the profession in both areas. One is Friedrich Gulda (1930-2000), who, in addition to his career as a virtuoso pianist, in 1962 began to cultivate jazz and improvisation. Another is Gunther Schuller (b.1925), composer, French horn player and author of *The Swing Era,* named 'jazz book of the century' by *Jazz Educators Journal.* Also to be mentioned are pianist, composer and Harvard academic Mel Powell (1923-1998), trombonist and composer Raymond Premru (b. 1934), pianist Keith Jarrett and bassist Richard Davis (b.1930). The British composer and pianist Richard Rodney Bennett (b.1936) sings a very convincing jazz ballad, but no major jazz singer seems to have succeeded in both categories. The very difficulty of compiling the above list makes the point.

Wynton Marsalis belongs to this rare elite. His achievement in bridging the divide between jazz and orchestral playing eclipses even those of Goodman and Previn. Not only was Wynton Marsalis the first musician ever to win Grammy awards in both jazz and classical categories, but, like all his other achievements, this was accomplished early in his life.

Wynton's emergence and first successes occurred at the start of the 1980s. The jazz style in which he played was rooted in the Blue Note music of the late 1950s and early 1960s. Miles Davis, who had so frequently pointed the way forward for jazz, and whose style from an earlier period was part of the music Marsalis emulated, now emerged from retirement with a straightforward fusion band, using synthesizers and rock rhythms, showing little sense of adventure or experiment.

In the late 1980s Wynton, with the critic (and former drummer) Stanley Crouch, began attacking Miles in print, saying that Miles had left jazz for the pop marketplace. The criticisms were outspoken, strongly expressed, and many regarded Wynton as too new on the scene, and, paradoxically, too much influenced by Miles Davis, for it to be seemly for him to say such things. Though there was more than a grain of truth in what Wynton was expressing, observers were reminded of the old advice about glass houses and stones. Wynton, though a wonderful trumpet player, was conservative in his approach to jazz, and at the time not yet a genuinely individual stylist.

After Wynton came a host of these 'young lions', also called 'yuppie jazz musicians', 'neo-bop', 'neoclassicists' or 'new conservatives'. They included Terence Blanchard, Roy Hargrove, Tom Harrell, Nicholas Payton and Wallace Roney on trumpets, James Carter, Kenny Garrett, Javon Jackson, Branford Marsalis, Joshua Redman and Gary Thomas (b.1961) on saxophones, and Cyrus Chestnut, Benny Green and Marcus Roberts on piano.

Eric Nisenson, who has written at length about this problematical aspect of contemporary jazz in *Blue: The Murder of Jazz,* says: "The emergence and promotion of these young musicians was supposed to be good for jazz, supposedly giving birth to this new 'golden era,' which is how a number of writers have described this period of jazz. But in the long run, of course, it was neither good for jazz nor good for these young jazz musicians to be declared masters when they were just at a point of beginning to learn what jazz is all about." [1]

The flames of this controversy were further fueled by the policy adopted by Wynton for his *Jazz at Lincoln Center* series, wherein he was widely accused of bias against white musicians. The controversy was renewed by the manner in which Wynton discharged his responsibilities as presenter and adviser for the major TV series, *Jazz,* produced by Ken Burns.

By design or coincidence, in 1999 the cornetist and author Richard Sudhalter published *Lost Chords, White Musicians and Their Contribution to Jazz, 1915-1945.* [2] Despite its title, this is not a contentious book. Sudhalter merely attempts to contest the increasingly held view of early white musicians as musically insignificant. This publication, thoroughly researched and engagingly written, is an obligatory read for anyone studying jazz up to the bebop era. It would be unfortunate if jazz were to become mired in a tug-of-war between revisionist views of jazz history based largely on race. Reverse racism is still racism.

Whatever else has been said about the work of Wynton Marsalis and the Lincoln Center Jazz Orchestra, there is no better introduction to jazz than to attend a concert by the band. Wynton, a charming and communicative bandleader, masterminds a disciplined and polished ensemble, with a deep sense of tradition, offering accessible performances that avoid the obscure or self indulgent.

185

The Lincoln Center Jazz Orchestra is not the only jazz ensemble to be part of an official organization and to receive official funding. In France, the Government has created the Orchestre National de Jazz (ONJ). Similar organizations supporting jazz orchestras, frequently linked to a broadcasting company, include the Danish Radio Band in Copenhagen, the Stockholm Jazz Orchestra in Sweden, the UMO Big Band in Finland, and the WDR Big Band in Cologne, Germany. Regrettably, there is no such ensemble in Britain, though the UK Jazz Development Trust has lobbied for the establishment of one.

Jazz Education

Of course, at first there were no written methods of instruction. Jazz was taught by example, whether by observing live performances in person, from recordings, or private study. The next generation - Louis Armstrong and his contemporaries - chose prominent New Orleans musicians as their ideals. Relatively few musicians were taken as models. These included Buddy Bolden, Bunk Johnson, Joe Oliver, Jelly Roll Morton and a handful of others. After 1917, recordings, and later the radio, served as the main medium of dissemination.

The influence of Louis Armstrong was enormous. Players taught themselves by listening to and copying from his records, memorizing key aspects of his style. During the 1920s and 1930s, sheet music collections of Armstrong's 'hot licks' were published. These were compilations of short phrases, taken out of context, usually without any harmonic information.

The jam sessions, rent parties and cutting contests created opportunities for musicians to learn from each other. By the time of the swing era there were available published collections of hot licks by other players, including those of Benny Goodman and Coleman Hawkins. Additionally, Goodman, Artie Shaw, Woody Herman, Harry

James and others published instrumental instruction books. It is not at all clear when the guitar chord symbol method of notating jazz harmony was codified and adopted. Many popular sheet music publications of the 1920s and 1930s carry ukulele chord box diagrams, which offer a harmonic shorthand.

Jazz activity began in American colleges as early as the 1920s, though ensembles were usually student initiated and student led, frequently playing little more than jazz-influenced dance music. However, at least one institution, Alabama State Normal College, had a jazz ensemble that was officially recognized by the end of the 1920s.

By the middle 1930s there were instructional columns appearing in jazz magazines, together with jazz transcriptions. The first arranging books were published. In major American cities, competent musicians who played jazz began to teach. Many of the leading swing musicians seemed hungry for knowledge and formal study. From the height of the swing period onward, several prominent jazz musicians explored classical music, and many turned to serious performers and composers to widen their education. Benny Goodman studied with classical clarinetist Reginald Kell, Charlie Parker pestered Edgard Varèse for lessons, Quincy Jones studied with legendary French teacher Nadia Boulanger. One notable figure sought out by several prominent jazzmen was Joseph Schillinger (1895 - 1943). He had left Russia in 1928, settled in New York, and taught music, mathematics, art history and his own rhythmic theories at the New School for Social Research, New York University, and Columbia University Teachers College.

Schillinger had devised a system of composition that reduced the elements of rhythm, melody and harmony to what he called 'geometric phase relationships'. Eventually, he expanded this idea to include orchestration, emotion in music, theater, design, and the moving image. Schillinger's system was taught to his private pupils. They included prominent musicians such as pianist Eubie Blake, trombonist Tommy Dorsey, Vernon Duke, George Gershwin, Benny Goodman, composer, pianist, actor and author Oscar Levant, John Lewis, Gerry Mulligan, and Glenn Miller.[3] Today, little mention is made of Schillinger's writings. Significantly, despite his grand theories he did not employ them in his own music. The Schillinger House of Music in Boston was founded by pianist and arranger Lawrence Berk in 1945. In 1954 Berk changed the name to Berklee College of Music.

In June, 1944, President Franklin D. Roosevelt signed the 'Servicemen's Readjustment Act of 1944,' better known as the 'G. I. Bill of Rights.' This law made available billions of dollars in education and training for millions of armed service veterans. It was famed legislation which has since been recognized as one of the most important acts of Congress. To this day, American men and women in uniform still earn education benefits. At the end of World War II, many service musicians entered higher education as a result of the bill. Institutions such as North Texas State University, the University of Miami and, later, Berklee College of Music, rose to prominence in this era, a period that effectively marked the beginning of the rise of formal jazz education in the USA.

Berklee alumni include guitarist John Abercrombie, the arranger Toshiko Akiyoshi, vibraphone player Gary Burton, guitarist Kevin Eubanks, arranger Quincy Jones, singer Diana Krall, saxophonist Branford Marsalis, producer/arranger Arif Mardin, guitarist Al DiMeola, saxophonist Scott Robinson, guitarist John Scofield, and saxophonists Sadao Watanabe and Ernie Watts.

As early as 1942, Leonard Feather, Marshall Stearns and Robert Goffin taught the first jazz history course, at the New School for Social Research in New York. During the 1950s many American colleges and universities added jazz studies to their list of courses. Music publishers began to offer graded band arrangements, and the first summer schools were held. The Stan Kenton big band camps were organized during this period. These later evolved into the Jamey Aebersold combo camps.

ABC of Jazz Education

Jamey Aebersold is the 'A' of the 'A B C' of jazz education. The 'B' is David Baker, the 'C' Jerry Coker. Baker is the widely published author of books on arranging and jazz improvisation, and Chair of the Jazz Department at Indiana University. Coker is a former Woody Herman saxophonist, author of several seminal texts on jazz pedagogy and Professor of Music at the University of Tennessee. Aebersold, a saxophonist and businessman, has had a great impact on jazz education. His series of 'play-along' records is a commercially available library of 'music minus one' of more than ninety CDs, covering many standard songs, jazz originals and Broadway tunes. In turn this inspired today's *Band in a Box* computer software, which effectively provides for jazz students to create their own play-along recording, in any key, at any tempo, with any chord progression.

In 1960 there were five thousand high school jazz bands in the USA. By the middle of that decade more than forty American colleges offered degrees in jazz studies. In 1968 Matt Betton (1913-2002) founded the National Association of Jazz Educators (NAJE), with a first year membership of a hundred. The name was changed to the International Association of Jazz Educators (IAJE) in the early 1990s, though even at the time of writing the membership is predominantly American. The annual conference (usually held in January) rarely takes place outside North America, though there are members in thirty-one countries. Today, education is an integral part of jazz. Jazz education has boomed. Now it is possible to study jazz to degree and postgraduate level in a college environment in many countries. In New York, J@LC is committed to jazz education. After another adjustment to its name, the International Association for Jazz Education now has in excess of eight thousand members, being the fastest growing music education organization in the world.

From the beginning, jazz was often attacked and derided. This was not merely the usual antipathy of the older generation towards the music of the youngsters, and it was not only the Nazis who banned jazz. The hostility was widespread. Jazz was belittled in music education texts and journals. It was thought to have a degenerative effect on school music. Around the world, many teachers of serious music banned jazz from being played in practice rooms. When pianist Roland Hanna (1932-2002) studied music at the Eastman School of Music, Rochester, he was forbidden to play jazz.[4]

The eminent classical violinist Nigel Kennedy (b. 1956) studied at the Juilliard School of Music in New York. Jazz violinist Stephane Grappelli was appearing at Carnegie Hall. Though his violin teacher Dorothy DeLay had told Kennedy not to play jazz, he went on stage with Grappelli. "Two days later, I was having a lesson with Dottie again...She then proclaimed that there had been two CBS A&R classical music people there and that as a result I'd never record classical music for that label because of that one jazz appearance."[5]

Attitudes began to change in the 1960s and 1970s, though not completely. As recently as 1980, the director of Leeds College of Music - which at that time possessed the largest jazz department in the UK - explicitly prohibited staff and students from playing jazz on the college's best piano! No reason was given.

Yet, very gradually, jazz was accepted by the music education community. This was partly because it came to be regarded as art music and not as mere dance music or entertainment. Jazz was also successful in attracting students. Extracurricular jazz activities were notably popular.

During the 1960s, jazz education began to take place outside America, first in Graz (Austria) and Leeds (UK), then in many countries. As the opportunities for a young instrumentalist to earn a living as a professional jazz musician, or as a sideman in a touring band, shrank, so the college jazz departments grew. The new jazz departments offered work to those older musicians who had the necessary communicative and pedagogical qualities to enable them to teach. In the context of poor employment prospects in the jazz profession it was possible (in the early years, when college places were not so plentiful) to recruit a student intake of talented young musicians.

By the mid-1970s to the early 1980s, the music education community began to accept jazz gracefully. In the new century, jazz education is generally considered to be a vital component of the study of music. The flow of students between countries became a two-way trend. At the time of writing over 40% of the students at Boston's Berklee College of Music are of foreign origin. In Europe, the International Association of Schools of Jazz (IASJ) flourishes. Jazz departments in Australia, Austria, Denmark, France, Germany, Holland, Israel and Britain have American staff and students. In Britain, the large, long-established commercial music examination organization, the Associated Board of the Royal Schools of Music (ABRSM) introduced local graded exams in jazz at the beginning of the new century. In 2003, the ABRSM examined more than 600,000 candidates worldwide. Many were sitting the new jazz syllabus. The eventual impact of this initiative on jazz education will be enormous.

Jazz education is not without its critics. Some commentators have pointed to an unhealthy concentration on music that originated between 1945 and 1965, the period from Parker to late Coltrane. Attending an IAJE conference (they are spectacular events), one finds that Dixieland is almost ignored, free jazz overlooked, and rock-jazz and funk relegated to a less prominent place in the curriculum. Many tutors seem to be guilty of an 'I'll teach what I love' attitude, and are seemingly embarrassed by early swing, New Orleans jazz and the avant-garde. Compromise is needed.

The new century has also seen the rise of a new breed of jazz scholar, who introduces the mysterious language of sociology, comparative literature, film studies and linguistic theory into homely jazz contexts. Ploughing through complex, opaque prose, one wonders what Louis Armstrong, Charlie Parker or Duke Ellington would have made of these developments.

The importance of education and understanding - even for the listener - has been vividly described in an analogy by journalist Sholto Byrnes. Imagine a man looking through a window high above a trampoline. "All he sees is a group of people bobbing up and down, seemingly at random. If he could see the trampoline, he would understand their movements, just as the listener needs to understand the chordal basis of a jazz improvisation to comprehend how the performer is using it." [6]

References

1. Nisenson, E., op. cit., p.226.
2. Sudhalter, R., op. cit.
3. Burk, J. M. and Schneider, W. J., *New Grove Dictionary of Music and Musicians*, Vol. 22 (London: Macmillan, 2001), p. 506.
4. Voce, S., *Roland Hanna*. Obituary in *The Independent*, London, 16 November, 2002.
5. Kennedy, N., *Always Playing* (London: Weidenfeld and Nicolson, 1991), p. 19.
6. Byrnes, S., *The Independent*, London, 30 May, 2003.

12. After 2000. The New Century Questions and Answers

Where Do I Start?

"Jazz is a music you count out at your own peril," wrote the critic Gary Giddins in 1999.[1] If you are relatively new to jazz, there are many wonderful instrumentalists whose performances are well worth seeking out, and there is much excellent critical writing to steer you through your discoveries.

The easiest way to hear as much jazz as you want is to listen via your computer. Many specialist jazz stations relay their programs online. Just type 'jazz on the web', 'Internet jazz', or a similar phrase on to a good search engine to find a list of jazz-only radio stations across the world. The BBC website offers a selection of recent jazz programs, accessible at any time.

Radio must not be forgotten, of course, although there is a limited number of jazz-carrying terrestrial stations, particularly on mainstream channels. Television is generally even more restricted than national radio in its jazz output, though there are exceptions, usually expensive. Availability of jazz on CD is excellent. Particularly recommended are the specialist secondhand jazz record shops, to be found in most large cities. The array of jazz on DVD, usually offered alongside CDs, is limited but improving.

Surely, the most important activity is to get out and hear some jazz live? That's how jazz is best appreciated, by seeing the interaction between players, to observe exactly how drummers do what they do, what pianists do with their feet, how mutes look and sound on brass instruments, and a thousand other things.

Listening to Jazz

You are what you hear! Musicians who teach music appreciation classes discover that most non-players hear music differently from competent instrumentalists. Those who play music must, to a greater or lesser extent, listen carefully and understand what they hear.

Not surprisingly, lay listeners usually hear music as a background, rather than hearing with comprehension and concentration. A handful of non-playing listeners will not even be able to distinguish between instruments. Incredibly, some people cannot tell whether a note goes up or goes down. Really! Some will not be able to separate a saxophone from a trumpet. Not many will be able to tell trumpet from cornet, or differentiate between tenor and baritone saxophones, or the violin from the viola. When it comes to considering jazz performances, or classical forms such as the sonata, many listeners will not perceive the 'shape' of the music, probably will not count bar lines or recognize the sections of the musical form. When hearing jazz, they may not be able to discriminate between theme statements and improvisation. Even fewer people have an ear for harmony. A keen listener once told me, "I first heard jazz as 'musical scribble'." Time was needed to appreciate the link between a soloist's notes and the underlying harmonies.

We live in an age when recorded music is constantly played as a background, in the supermarket, in airports, bookshops, restaurants, public toilets, on the phone when you are put on hold, and even listened to by students when they are reading. Under these circumstances it is impossible to attend carefully. Start listening to jazz under conditions where you can give the music your full attention. Take a tip from serious musicians, some of whom will have spent thousands of hours learning to analyze what they hear. Most find it impossible to focus *properly* on music while they are doing something else that requires concentration. Not for them the enjoyment of a symphony while they are driving the car in heavy traffic, or the pleasure of a string quartet while reading a novel. No jazz plays in *their* CD drive (or on the Internet!) while they are working at the computer. Under any of these conditions, for them, music is heard rather than listened to.

Stop Listening!

The effect of this constant onslaught of music is that we become immune to its effect. We stop listening attentively. So the first suggestion for sharpening up your listening skills is to avoid using jazz as a background to other activities, or as a way of creating a mood or atmosphere. This is not to disapprove of atmospheric music, but it teaches you very little. Organize listening sessions where you pay attention. Listen less frequently, but listen more carefully.

Fortunately, there are many high spots of jazz on record. They represent some of the most entrancing moments of twentieth-century music. Discovering these wonderful performances will be a pleasure.

What Do I Listen For?

Begin by identifying the instruments. Can you name them all? Distinguish the alto saxophone from the tenor saxophone, or trumpet from cornet. Check to see if you were right. Do not be disappointed if you get it wrong. It is not easy. Soon you will be able to identify famous individual players.

Next, pay attention to what each instrument does. Is the bass playing two in a bar, or four - or something else? Which parts of his kit is the drummer using? What are the cymbals doing? Is the drummer playing with sticks, brushes or bare hands? Are the brass players using mutes? Listen for vibrato. If it is well done, it is often not noticed.

Then try to analyze the musical role of each instrument. Counting the number of trumpets, trombones or saxophones is worthwhile, often impossible on a recording, simple at a concert. After a performance, try asking fellow listeners how many instruments they saw on stage. Quickly you will understand how easy it is for listeners to be unobservant.

Are the reeds playing above or below the brass? If it is a combo or big band, listen for playing in unison, when instruments play the same notes as distinct from playing in harmony. How is the piano interacting with the rhythm section? In what way is the pianist using his or her left hand? Where does the guitar fit in?

Pay attention to what the music is doing. Count along to check the underlying pulse. Is it two, three, four or even five, or more. Count through drum solos. They are mostly in multiples of four bars - eight, twelve, sixteen bars, and so on. Consider the form of the music. Most likely it will be written in cycles of twelve bars, or thirty-two bars, but not always. Can you recognize any changes of key?

The Instruments of Jazz

Musical instruments are traditionally divided into four families: woodwind, brass, strings and percussion. Today, a fifth family could be added, that of electronic instruments.

As jazz evolved from the marching band, from work song, Negro spirituals, European dance forms and several other ingredients, instrumental jazz tended to use the so-called outdoor instruments, the noisier ones, particularly the readily available wind and percussion instruments. This explains the predominance of clarinets and saxophones (woodwind), trumpets and trombones (brass), and drums (percussion), throughout jazz.

However, almost all musical instruments have been used in jazz at some time. Fats Waller recorded jazz on the church organ. The harpsichord, expertly played by Johnny Guarnieri, was an important ingredient of the sound of Artie Shaw's Gramercy Five. Rufus Harley played jazz on the bagpipes, Ron McCroby has whistled jazz, Phil Bodner added the English horn (cor anglais) to Oliver Nelson's band, Toots Thielemans plays wonderful jazz harmonica, and Don Ellis brought elements of the Balinese gamelan to his jazz orchestra.

Nevertheless, some of the characteristics of jazz are more suited to certain instruments. The wind instruments used most frequently are those which can take on the personality of the player, and those which can achieve a vocal quality in the tone produced. This explains why the saxophone has been such a popular instrument in jazz and why, for example, the flute, the oboe and the French horn are less popular.

Much of the best jazz has contained an element of audacity, humor, sauciness, rebellion, or even outrage. Jazz frequently relies on some sort of angst to fuel it. Novelist Stephen King once observed that humor is almost always anger with its makeup on. He may well have been thinking of some jazz performances when he made that remark. The impertinence, the vulgarity, was there at the beginning of recorded jazz, in the barnyard effects of the ODJB, with cornet imitations of a horse whinnying, and whooping effects on the clarinet. How could you describe Jelly Roll Morton's inclusion of car klaxons and spoken interjections in his Red Hot Pepper performances? Guerrilla theater before its time, maybe.

Jelly is widely portrayed as having elephantiasis of the ego, knowing more about lights than bushels (he claimed to have invented jazz in 1901), but his tracks from 1927/8 are wonderful, not to be missed. The audacity persists in Duke Ellington's jungle music at the Cotton Club in Harlem or, more subtly, in Duke's later exploitation of the clicking sound made by Russell Procope's broken clarinet key. Ornette

Coleman's decision to make a recording playing the violin, only weeks after taking up this most difficult of instruments, is part of the same phenomenon, as are the theatrical performances of Sun Ra and the Art Ensemble of Chicago.

Certain instruments are more suitable than others for this radical role. The trombone, with its music hall associations, lends itself well to impudence. Likewise the saxophone. The boldness of using found objects - glass tumblers or plumbers' rubber plungers - as brass mutes, is also part of this brashness or impertinence. Again, the effects achieved often mimic the human voice.

Is Improvisation Just 'Making It Up'?

How can one tell if improvisation is brand-new? Unless you hear the same player on several consecutive nights, playing the same material, you are unlikely to know whether a solo is improvised anew on each performance or whether the player is a mere lickmeister. Does it matter? Good improvisation is akin to talking, saying something. Surely the essential point is that jazz *sounds* improvised, just like conversation? A good analogy exists in stand-up comedy. A professional comedian sounds as though he is thinking aloud, making it up as he goes along. Yet if you have his routine on tape, and listen to it repeatedly, you realize there are few superfluous words, the act has been carefully polished. Much repetition of that performance has brought it to such a fluent standard. So it is with jazz. We have evidence that some of the greatest players did not always improvise fresh solos. When he was young, American saxophonist Bob Wilber studied extensively with Sidney Bechet. He discovered that Bechet would prepare and memorize a couple of choruses of 'improvisation' on items in his repertoire. Then, when performing, he had something ready to play as a climax after completing several choruses of genuine improvisation, something prepared in case he was feeling tired or unwell, or was in other difficult circumstances. Naturally, he didn't publicize the existence of this 'boil in a bag' jazz. To him it was all part of being a professional.

Duke Ellington once remarked that no one played anything worth hearing if he had not thought about it before, whether that thought took place one minute before or one week before.

Others hold a vehemently opposite opinion, arguing that the joy in jazz improvisation lies in exploration, and that the act of taking a chance in front of an audience is the whole point of what they do. This is an idealist's view, often expressed by those who have not put themselves in the place of the touring jazz musician who is expected to come up with something compelling under the most trying circumstances.

Indeed, if improvisation were totally fresh, we would probably not be able to recognize the player. When we listen to a jazz trombonist, how do we know whether we are hearing Jack Teagarden or Rob McConnell? The answer is because we recognize the tone, pitch, vibrato, tessitura (how high or how low the majority of notes lie within a given range), tonguing and repertoire. But there are also trademark phrases which occur repeatedly with all players. Even the great saxophone genius Charlie Parker has a repertoire, albeit very large, of favorite and instantly recognized licks and phrases.

Why Is Someone Historically Important?

Musicians are held to be historically important when they bring something new to the genre, when they appear to be a significant influence on those who follow, when they change the course of history. However, it is very easy to make assumptions about influences, not so easy to be certain that the assumptions are correct. A horse and a sheep both feed solely on grass, take in the rays of the sun, drink only water. In this respect their 'influences' are the same. Yet how different they look and sound. Only a fool would say, "This part of the sheep is due to the rays of the sun, and this characteristic of the horse is due to grass."

In jazz, even the players themselves are not always sure why they sound the way they do. For instance, there is a consensus that tenor saxophonist Lester Young influenced Charlie Parker. Young is also said to have influenced Stan Getz. Yet Getz and Parker sound entirely different. Prez did inspire both of them, to be sure, but there were other puissant influences operating. Spotting those is part of the fun.

References

1.   Giddins, G., op.cit., p. xiii.

Select Bibliography

Abe, K. *Jazz Giants. A Visual Retrospective*. New York: Billboard Publications, 1988.

Adams, Simon. *Jazz, A Crash Course*. London: Simon and Schuster, 1999.

Atkins, Ronald, ed. *All That Jazz*. London: Carlton Books, 1996.

Baron, Stanley. *Benny, King of Swing*. London: Thames and Hudson, 1979.

Bechet, Sidney. *Treat it Gentle*. London: Corgi Books, 1964.

Berendt, Joachim. *The Jazz Book*. London: Paladin Books, 1989.

Bergerot, Frank and Merlin, Arnaud. *The Story of Jazz - Bop and Beyond*. London: Thames & Hudson, 1991.

Berliner, Paul. *Thinking in Jazz*. Chicago: University of Chicago Press, 1994.

Blieck, Rob van der, ed. *The Thelonious Monk Reader*. New York: OUP, 2001.

Carner, Gary. *The Miles Davis Companion*. London: Omnibus Press, 1996.

Carr, Ian. *Keith Jarrett. The Man and his Music*. London: Grafton Books, 1991.

Carr, Ian, Fairweather, Digby, Priestley, Brian. *Jazz: The Essential Companion*. London: Paladin, 1987.

Carr, Roy. *A Century of Jazz*. London: Octopus Publishing, 1999.

Carver, R. and Bernstein, L. *Jazz Profiles*. New York: Billboard Books, 1998.

Case, Brian, and Britt, Stan. *The Illustrated Encyclopedia of Jazz*. London: Salamander Books, 1978.

Chilton, J. *The Song of the Hawk*. London: Quartet Books, 1990.

Collier, James Lincoln. *Benny Goodman and the Swing Era*. New York: OUP, 1989.

Condon, Eddie. *We Called it Music*. London: Corgi Books, 1962.

Cook, R. and Morton, B. *The Penguin Guide to Jazz on CD*. London: Penguin Books, 2002.

Cooke, Mervyn. *Jazz*. London: Thames and Hudson, 1998.

Cooke, M. and Horn, D. *The Cambridge Companion to Jazz*. Cambridge University Press, 2002.

Coryell, J. and Friedman, L. *Jazz-Rock Fusion*. London: Marion Boyars, 1978.

Crouch, Stanley. *The All-American Skin Game: On the Corner: The Sellout of Miles Davis*. New York: Random House, 1995.

Crumpacker, B. and Crumpacker, C. *Jazz Legends*. Layton, Utah: Gibbs Smith, 1995.

Dankworth, J. *Jazz In Revolution*. London: Constable and Company, 1999.

Davis, Miles, with Troupe, Quincy. *Miles, The Autobiography*. London: Picador, 1989.

Easton, C. *Straight Ahead, the Story of Stan Kenton.* New York: Morrow, 1973.

Encyclopedia Britannica. Chicago: Encyclopedia Britannica, 2003.

Fairweather, D. *Notes from a Jazz Life.* London: Northway Publications, 2002.

Firestone, Ross. *Swing, Swing, Swing. The Life and Times of Benny Goodman.* London: Hodder and Stoughton, 1993.

Fisher, L., ed. *Jazz Research Proceedings Yearbook.* Manhattan, Kansas: IAJE Publications, 2001.

Fisher, L. *Miles Davis and Dave Liebman: Jazz Connections.* Ceredigion: Edwin Mellen Press, 1996.

Freeman, B. *Crazeology.* Oxford: Bayou Press, 1989.

Gabbard, K., ed. *Jazz Among the Discourses.* Durham: Duke University Press, 1995.

Gabbard, K., ed. *Representing Jazz.* Durham: Duke University Press, 1995.

Gelly, Dave. *Masters of Jazz Saxophone.* London: Balafon Books, 2000.

Giddins, Gary. *Riding on a Blue Note.* New York: Da Capo Press, 2000.

Gioia, Ted. *West Coast Jazz.* University of California Press, 1998.

Goddard, Chris. *Jazz Away from Home.* New York: Paddington Press, 1979.

Goffin, Robert. *Jazz, from Congo to Swing.* London: Musicians Press Ltd., 1946.

Gottlieb, Robert, ed. *Reading Jazz.* London: Bloomsbury Publishing, 1997.

Graham, Charles, and Morgenstern, Dan. *The Great Jazz Day.* California: Woodford Press, 2000.

Green, Benny. *Such Sweet Thunder.* London: Schirmer, 2001.

Gridley, M. C. *Jazz Styles: History and Analysis.* 8th ed. New Jersey: Prentice Hall, 2000.

Ingram, Adrian. *A Concise History of the Electric Guitar.* Pacific, Missouri: Mel Bay Publications, 2001.

Jones, Max. *Jazz Talking: profiles, interviews, and other riffs on jazz musicians.* Boulder, Colorado : Da Capo Press, 2000.

Jost, E. *Free Jazz.* New York: Da Capo Press, 1994.

Kahn, Ashley. *Kind of Blue. The Making of a Miles Davis Masterpiece.* London: Granta Publications, 2000.

Kernfeld, Barry, ed. *The New Grove Dictionary of Jazz.* New York: The Macmillan Press Limited, 1994.

King, J. *What Jazz Is.* London: Penguin Books, 1998.

Knight, Richard. *The Blues Highway. New Orleans to Chicago.* Hindhead, Surrey:

Trailblazer Publications, 2001.

Laubich, Arnold, and Spencer, Ray. *Art Tatum, a Guide to his Recorded Music*. Metuchen, New Jersey: Scarecrow Press, 1982.

Lawn, R. J., and Helmer, J. L. *Jazz Theory and Practice*. Belmont, California: Wadsworth Publishing Company, 1993.

Lawson, C., ed. *The Cambridge Companion to the Clarinet*. Cambridge University Press, 1995.

Lees, Gene. *Meet Me at Jim & Andy's*. Oxford: Oxford University Press, 1988.

Lees, Gene. *Arranging the Score*. London: Cassell, 2000.

Levinson, Peter. *Trumpet Blues, The Life of Harry James*. New York: OUP, 1999.

Levinson, Peter. *September in the Rain. The Life of Nelson Riddle*. New York: Billboard Books, 2001.

Mathieson, K. *Giant Steps*. Edinburgh: Payback Press, 1999.

Mezzrow, Mezz. *Really The Blues*. London: Corgi Books, 1961.

Mingus, Charles, ed. Nel King. *Beneath the Underdog: His World as Composed by Mingus*. New York: Random House, 1971 (Reprint Vintage, 1991).

Morgenstern, Dan. *Jazz People*. New York: Da Capo Press, 1993.

Nicholson, S. *Jazz, The Modern Resurgence*. London: Simon and Schuster, 1990.

Nisenson, Eric. *Blue, the Murder of Jazz*. New York: Da Capo Press, 2000.

Owens, Thomas. *Bebop, The Music and the Players*. New York: OUP, 1995.

Placksin, Sally. *Jazz Women*. London: Pluto Press, 1985.

Rattenbury, Ken. *Duke Ellington, Jazz Composer*. New Haven: Yale University Press, 1990.

Reisner, Robert. *Bird: The Legend of Charlie Parker*. London: MacGibbon and Kee, 1962.

Schoenberg, Loren. *The NPR Curious Listener's Guide to Jazz*. New York: Perigree Books, 2002.

Schuller, Gunther. *Early Jazz*. New York: OUP, 1968.

Schuller, Gunther. *The Swing Era*. New York: OUP, 1989.

Shadwick, Keith. *Bill Evans. Everything Happens to Me*. San Francisco: Backbeat Books, 2002.

Shapiro, N., and Hentoff, N. *Hear Me Talkin' to Ya*. London: Souvenir Press, 1992.

Shaw, Artie. *The Trouble With Cinderella*. New York: Da Capo Press, 1979.

Shipton, Alyn. *A New History of Jazz*. London: Continuum, 2001.

Smith, G. *Stéphane Grappelli*. London: Pavilion Books, 1987.

Spencer, Frederick J. *Jazz and Death*. University of Mississippi Press, 2002.

Stokes, W. Royal. *The Jazz Scene*. New York: OUP, 1991.

Stokes, W. Royal. *Living the Jazz Life*. New York: OUP, 2000.

Sudhalter, Richard M. *Lost Chords. White Musicians and their Contribution to Jazz, 1915-1945*. New York: OUP, 1999.

Tucker, M. *The Duke Ellington Reader*. New York: OUP, 1993.

Turro, Frank. *Jazz, A History*. New York: W. W. Norton, 1993.

Yanow, S. *Bebop*. San Francisco: Miller Freeman Books, 2000.

Yanow, S. *Classic Jazz*. San Francisco: Backbeat Books, 2001.

Zammarchi, Fabrice and Mas, Sylvie. *A Life in the Golden Age of Jazz. A Biography of Buddy DeFranco*. Seattle: Parkside Publications, 2002.

Index

210

215